New Moon
at Batoche

New Moon
at Batoche

GEORGE MELNYK

REFLECTIONS ON THE
URBAN PRAIRIE

THE BANFF CENTRE
PRESS

CANADIAN CATALOGUING IN PUBLICATION DATA

Melnyk, George.
New moon at Batoche.
ISBN 0-920159-67-2

1. Prairie Provinces. 2. Regionalism–Prairie Provinces. I. Title.
FC3237.M44 1999   971.2' 08   C99-911245-7
F1060.M438 1999

Edited by Richard Harrison

DESIGN AND COVER PHOTOGRAPH BY VANGOOL DESIGN + TYPOGRAPHY, CALGARY
PRINTED AND BOUND IN CANADA BY FRIESENS, ALTONA, MANITOBA

The Banff Centre Press gratefully acknowledges the support of the Canada Council for the Arts for its publishing program.

Le Conseil des Arts   The Canada Council
du Canada   for the Arts

THE BANFF CENTRE
FOR THE ARTS

BANFF CENTRE PRESS

Box 1020–17, Banff, Alberta, Canada T0L 0C0
http://www.banffcentre.ab.ca/Writing/Press

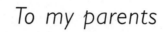

To my parents

Acknowledgements

The author would like to thank the Alberta Foundation for the Arts for the financial assistance of a Senior Writers Grant while he was preparing this manuscript. Richard Harrison, who edited the text for the Banff Centre Press, was a sensitive and thoughtful editor. An initial version of "Why I Am Not a Good Ukrainian: A Family Fable" was a speech to the members of The Ukrainian Canadian Professional Business Club in Calgary. "The Urban Prairie: Between Jerusalem and Babylon" was an address given at a Glenbow Museum lecture series.

Previously published material
in this volume:

"Identity and the Western Writer" first appeared in *Freelance* (vol. 27, no. 4) Jan./Feb.1998, the newsletter of the Saskatchewan Writers Guild. It was the 1997 Caroline Heath Memorial Lecture.

"The Five City-States of the West" was first published in *The Urban Prairie* by Dan Ring, Guy Vanderhaeghe and George Melnyk (Saskatoon: Mendel Art Gallery and Fifth House Publishers, 1993). It is reprinted here with the kind permission of the publisher.

"Coming to Matador" was first published as "Matador: The Co-operative Farming Tradition" in Occasional Paper #92-02 (Saskatoon: Centre for the Study of Co-operatives, 1992). It is reprinted here in a revised form with the kind permission of the publisher.

"The Poet" was first published in *Ribstones* by George Melnyk (Victoria: Ekstasis Editions, 1996). It is reprinted here with the kind permission of the publisher.

Table of Contents

Preface 13

Heidegger at Batoche:
Postmodernism in Western Canadian Writing 19

I Am Butler:
Notes for an Autobiographical Long Poem 31

Identity and the Western Writer:
Literary Objects and Literary Saints 51

Why I Am Not a Good Ukrainian:
A Family Fable 71

The Five City-States of the West:
A Prairie Fantasy 85

The Urban Prairie:
Between Jerusalem and Babylon 103

Coming to Matador:
Dreams of the Soil 117

On Being a Self-styled Guru of Western Regionalism:
An Untrue Confession 133

Rivers of the Mind:
Praying to Water 145

Preface

YEARS AGO I WAS DRIVING WITH A FRIEND FROM Winnipeg to Edmonton in my white VW van, Heffalump. This was in the days when I regularly journeyed across the prairies to promote *NeWest ReView*, a magazine I had recently founded. It was dusk in central Saskatchewan when we turned off Highway 16 onto Highway 2 and headed north to Batoche. This was to be my first and only visit to the shrine where aboriginal identity and Western Canadian rebellion and protest are so deeply rooted.

It was dark when we arrived at Batoche National Historic Park on the South Saskatchewan River. Alone and under a full moon we spent a brief time examining and then gently touching the bullet holes in the walls. The mood of the place first wrapped around my imagination, then penetrated my mind with its total presence. The ghosts who played out the second act of Western Canada's political martyrdom were still here. I could feel them inside me.

On returning to Heffalump, white like the buildings, I looked up and noticed that an eclipse of the moon was underway. I took it to be a sign from the spirits of the place, whose faces I had seen in the silver tincture and glass plates of ancient photographs. A sign of what? I did not know. For me it was a new, trans-formed moon. Only many years later did it seem appropriate to com-memorate that event in naming this book. In spite of the physical reality of this book and its printed text, the narrative itself belongs more to Batoche that night and its elusive World of spir-its, imagination and fantasy than to the world of non-fiction, bodies, real objects and the solidity of the earth. Although this book seems full of daylight it really belongs to the reflective power of the blackened moon at Batoche.

I have searched my diaries from the period to confirm what happened that night but I have found nothing. Is it just a dream that haunts me? Did it really happen? Was it only a cloud that half-obscured the moon? Was I really there? I've lost touch with the friend who was the only witness that could confirm or deny the eclipse and the visit itself. So I have only memory. No matter how strong my memory is of having been there, I doubt my own recollection. The result is the kind of uncertainty we feel when what we have seen is suddenly lost to darkness and we proceed cautiously, simultaneously trusting and distrusting.

The project of this book is rooted in the essential ambiguity that haunts all recollection, speculation, dreaming, personal history and memory. A narrative of recollection pretends to put the writerly self together, to create the seemingly solid presence of a figure standing in a real landscape, but this is illusion. The flow of life's events, the unending parade of emotions, crises and epiphanies may be the inspiration for a text that claims to be "personal," but what does that really mean in terms of truth? The truth of the subject is much different from the truth of the object, and a book is an object. So the truth conveyed by a personal subject who turns truth into an object, like a book, is a truth that falls silently into a chasm. The most the reader can expect is half-truths. An eclipse allows us to see in a new, out-of-the-ordinary way, like seeing with a hand over one eye.

One thing that I am sure of is that this is the concluding volume of a trilogy whose narrative seeks to wrap up three decades of essay-writing while living in Alberta. The alpha point—*Radical Regionalism* (1981)—collected essays from the seventies. The mid-point, *Beyond Alienation* (1993), had as its focus the writings of the eighties. The omega point—*New Moon at Batoche*—expresses the experiences of the nineties. The link between the three books also has three strands: the spirit of contemporary Western Canada as I experienced it; my personal ideology of regionalism; and the personal identity I brought with me when I migrated from my ethnic home in Winnipeg to the shores of urban Alberta. Together they create a text surrounded by the beckoning wilderness of interpretation that we all enter with fear and excitement. When a writer is writing a book he is more than the thing he is creating, but when the book is published it stands above him, superior and irrevocable. In speaking the personal, he surrenders some of his mystery.

The millennium is more a vantage point for looking back than it is for looking forward into the new century. Although we possess a surfeit of historical knowledge, the past seems more and more like some great mystery in which we are increasingly lost, wandering from one significance to another, unable to create a clear path that leads somewhere definite. Today the knowledge and wisdom found in the print culture of "Gutenberg's Galaxy" has become a subordinate category to that of all-powerful electronic information. A book of essays is old-fashioned. It will not help you get a job, improve your sex life or make money. It will not even help you become a happier person. It is generally useless, except to those who enjoy the power of words or intellectual pleasure for its own sake.

Trilogies themselves have certain disturbing overtones because of their claim to have a beginning, a middle and an end, a supposedly straight line of rational intention from one volume to the other. In reality this imagined line is simply a retrospective creation after the fact. When I did the first book of essays no trilogy was intended. It was simply the collecting of what had been. Only when the second volume came out did the possibility of there being a trilogy first appear. But it was only after the writing of this third volume was complete that the trilogy came into existence. As a result the claim that this is the concluding volume of a trilogy has a *post factum* quality, a naming dependent on hindsight. Why is that important? Simply because so much of naming, such as designating three books a trilogy, is a recognition that something unified has come into being, when this was not the motivation for even one of the numerous essays in the trilogy. Naming, like the naming that happened to this book, comes later on when an object needs to be placed and made concentric with our expectations and cultural values. Naming means closure.

Three books and three continuous decades of life in Western Canada have produced a dialectical cycle of thesis, antithesis and synthesis. The first volume was full of hope and promise, like the beginning of some military campaign in which victory is the only expectation. That was the tone that imbued *Radical Regionalism*. The second decade was a time of disillusionment and resentment as the promise and vigour of the first decade (the seventies) began to ebb away in an age of mediocrity in which the political likes of Don Getty and Grant Devine replaced province-builders like Peter Lougheed and Alan Blakeney. So *Beyond Alienation* had an air of defeat about it. The third decade has turned out to be one of personal acceptance of the region's identity (both negative and positive) and a rediscovery of ways to connect with that identity beyond politics and social change. I have found a new importance in the land and its rivers. Thoughts about how to be-at-home in the West of large cities are at the fore. A new playfulness with identity and writing has surfaced and a strong sense of underlying continuity suggests the possibility of peace of mind, learning to accept what cannot be changed.

The ongoing insights of prairie writers into the regional world, the liberating temptations of postmodernism, the fullness and joy of urban life, the struggle with identities given and taken away, the autobiographical self-understanding that creates a personal hermeneutic, and the paradigms provided in childhood are just some of the elements, occasionally contradictory, that wander through this narrative.

In the postmodernist moment that has seized the regional imagination, authors must glean meanings from anywhere and everywhere; they must construct passionate universes and then deconstruct them with the same energy; they must absorb the verities of electronic information and its global orality like mother's milk and then regurgitate arcaneness—the printed word. The old rationalities and certainties about the region that first infused the minds of the generation formed prior to the contemporary period have been replaced by the new values and beliefs of the Information Age. As a member of that earlier generation I represent a doorway to the past and an acknowledgement of passage but in an echoing voice that the new generation may understand—the voice of mythology and re-created history, which entertains as casually as a video.

George Melnyk, *Calgary*

Heidegger at Batoche:

Postmodernism in Western Canadian Writing

TWENTY YEARS AGO I PUBLISHED A SHORT ESSAY titled "On Originality."[1] The essay concluded with the claim that an original Western Canadian style in the arts could only come about when "a liberated historical reality" freed the region from its colonial and neocolonial identity.[2] Unless this occurred those who were trying to create an indigenous Western Canadian expression would be doomed to failure because of the region's history of imitating art from the metropolitan centre. The model for my thinking was the experience of the Mexican Revolution of 1910 to 1920, which inspired the Mexican muralists to create a political art for their people that combined European aesthetics, socialist ideology and the monumental art of the Aztec empire. The muralists created an aesthetic that had not been seen before, and so theirs could truly be considered an indigenous Mexican contribution to the visual arts of the twentieth century.

About the same time, I was delivering a series of lectures on Western Canadian writing at a summer school held at the University of Lethbridge. These lectures dealt with women in prairie literature, the critics of Western Canadian writing, ethnicity, and the aboriginal world as understood by Eurocentric male writers. I have kept the yellowed sheets of my handwritten and typed talks. They now confront me in the same accusatory way that the essay on originality does. What has happened during the past two decades? Has anything changed? Of course, history moves forward but are the fundamental parameters different?

The region's imitative practice has continued just as it has also continued to produce new, accomplished writers. But the lack of a liberating historical change in the region's political or social status in Confederation has meant that its writers have reflected rather than influenced trends in world literature. The inherent dependency and hinterland status of the West remains. The latest wave of global thinking to affect the writers of the region has been the ideas and values of postmodernism. My first contact with the concept came in the 1970s when I interviewed Robert Kroetsch, the novelist and poet. In that decade he was still teaching at the State University of New York at Binghamton and guest lecturing and teaching creative writing in Western Canada during the summers. He later became a professor in the Department of English at the University of Manitoba. (In the mid-1990s he retired to Victoria.) While at Binghamton he had become co-editor of *Boundary II*, a journal that espoused post-modernism under the direction of the philosopher and literary critic William Spanos.

Kroetsch talked enthusiastically about this new philosophy and its contribution to writing. He mentioned Spanos frequently and Spanos's interest in the work of the twentieth-century German philosopher Martin Heidegger, whose thinking was an inspiration for the postmodernists as they sought to deconstruct and reconstruct language and meaning. I was curious about this because I had specialized in Heidegger while I was a graduate student in philosophy at the University of Toronto and had continued in later years to try to comprehend his generally incomprehensible writings. To think that the ideas of Martin Heidegger, a former associate of the Nazis, and arguably the greatest European philosopher of the twentieth century, should have an influence on Western Canadian writing simply amazed me. But this interaction between the universal (Heidegger and postmodernism) and the particular (Western Canadian writing) via the mediation of academic life in the imperial heartland of New York State seemed to me to be the perfect paradigm for how a colonized hinterland creates culture. Robert Kroetsch, so deeply rooted in Alberta and yet trained far from its cultural markers, was the right emissary for this literary thought.

The postmodernist mission to remake culture by remaking language and story suited the times. The main target for postmodernism is "narrative" and how it affects or creates "a text." A traditional narrative is a story with a beginning, a middle and an end. In the postmodernist universe this form of narrative and text has been attacked as inherently false and misleading. Postmodernists argue that it is Heidegger who taught us to view narrative as both fundamental to the human organization of experience and as a product of history. Critics of postmodernism claim that it is an ideology that is anti-communitarian, anti-historical and anti-place. And yet, it was Kroetsch's poetry of the 1970s, beginning with the chapbook *The Ledger* (1975) that broke new ground in Western Canadian poetry by adopting all the juxtapositioning, reinterpreting and skilful juggling of memory essential to the postmodernist sensibility. Although poetry is generally an elite experience in our society Kroetsch's subject matter—his pioneer family documents—is an elegy to the past that could be read and appreciated by most everyone. When he writes in the poem, "you must see / the confusion again / the chaos again / the original forest / under the turning wheel / the ripened wheat, the / razed forest, the wrung / man," he is presenting a world with our pioneer selves at the centre.

Juxtaposing the elitism of poetry and the populism of farm ledgers was Kroetsch's way of bringing the postmodernist quest to Western Canada. The deconstruction of such secular icons as the settler, whether in Ontario or Western Canada, frees the writer and the reader to reconceive the historical universe and his or her personal connection to the images that universe has preserved for us.

Breaking down language so that it will stop being one-dimensional is not just poetry's task but technology's and culture's as well. The importance of linguistic conflict to Western Canadian identity is evident when we look back at the battle of Batoche as the quintessential historical and mythic event in Western Canadian culture. What language or languages were spoken there? On the winning side it was Victorian colonial English. On the losing side it was French *patois,* frontier American English, Latin and Cree. The differing languages resulted in conflicting narratives coming out of the event, with French language narratives supportive of rebellion and English language narratives condemning it. The Cree narratives of injustice were not written down and remained in the oral tradition.

So at the very core of the Western Canadian identity are competing narratives as old as the seminal events of that identity. This multicultural, multilingual, multiracial reality is a perfect arena in which to play the postmodernist card, to bring, as it were, Heidegger to Batoche and re-adjust the power relations among narratives. There is infinite space in the myth and history of Batoche in which to explore the Western Canadian self. At

Batoche we can lose, find, re-invent, blend, and re-create that Western self over and over again. The myth of Batoche is radically open-ended and in that sense eternal. If Heidegger is the symbol for the universality of postmodernism, then Batoche is the metaphor for our particular engagement with it.

Celebrating the diversity of cultures, languages and meanings not only fits the general postmodernist ethic and understanding but also fits the populist-elitist dichotomy in regional narrative. The texts of Robert Kroetsch, Myrna Kostash, Aritha van Herk and Fred Wah are at play on the fields at Batoche because they partake of diversity and because they inhabit the populist-elitist dichotomy. Each of these writers struggles with the tension of opposites and what it means to be a Western Canadian writer at the end of the twentieth century. Their words are bullets lodged in the wood and plastered walls of our culture.

Let us begin with English, the great imperial language of this century, in which each of them writes. It is not their language in a total sense. Each one of them has another language and another narrative in their hearts: for Kroetsch it is German; for Kostash Ukrainian, for van Herk Dutch, and for Wah it is Chinese. The conflict of languages drives each of these Western Canadian writers. Their use of English contains ethnic identity, immigrant consciousness, other national identities and particular historical preoccupations, which are the opposite of those of the imperial language they use. Although English may have been their *lingua franca* from childhood, their identities were formed in a milieu that was not English in origin, giving each one of them a certain sense of linguistic and cultural outsideness. What they are saying to us in English carries the hidden influences of Cantonese or Ukrainian or German cultures. For them English is the great filter that obscures their roots and pretends to make them one, when they are actually many. Only by struggling to bend the conventions of the English language to their particular ethnic and cultural roots can they feel at home. To achieve this they must deconstruct, somehow create a "new" English language.

Canada's pre-eminent man of letters, George Woodcock, wrote in the early nineties that the "deconstructionist study of literature, which breaks down barriers of form and function... calls the reader into the heart of the process of creation and criticism."[3] By entering the heart of literary creation we eschew a system of rationality associated with the mind and enter the heart of postmodernism, a system of feeling and irrationality, of sewing pieces together that don't fit on the surface but make sense underneath because that is where unresolved conflicts reside. Since we live in an era of systemic deconstruction, the major one being the collapse of the Soviet Union and the end of a half-century of the Cold War, literary politics tends to fragment as well. These four writers are essentially political in their work—van Herk in her literary feminism, Kostash in her ethnic politics, Wah in his poetic search for a non-English English voice and Kroetsch in his deconstructivist celebration of the libido. Each adapts the English language to these goals. The postmodernist project suits them because it allows them to experiment with and escape the confines of strict modernity with its singular values and unquestioning assumptions, which the postmodernists see as cultural imperialism.

Woodcock makes the point that history is plausible fiction.[4] Kroetsch seeks to erase that historical plausibility by suggesting that history is more fiction than fact. If historical writing is represented by Herodotus and myth is represented by Homer, then Kroetsch stands with Homer. The philosopher Heidegger also stood with the poets against the historians when he described the right way of being in the world as the stance of *poesis.* He wrote extensively about the hidden meanings in Holderlin's poetry because he privileged the poet's personal insight over the historian's. This is true also in the case of Myrna Kostash, whose non-fiction classic *All of Baba's Children* sought to revise the ethnic past and historical myths that her community took for granted. Her emphasis on the personal point of view over collective correctness was an acknowledgement of the postmodernist perspective: what is mine is truth, the whole truth and nothing but the truth whatever lies it may contain. What is given must be retaken and remoulded, so that we can live with ourselves.

Hermeneutics is the theory of interpretation. The philosopher Paul Ricoeur is its main proponent. He talks about "discourse" and "voice" and metaphoric truth. He says that "metaphor destroys an order only to invent a new one."[5] The order created by metaphor is the order of myth. All orders imposed on the world, both private and public, singular and collective, are mythic, so when the postmodernist seeks to deconstruct an order, the result is a new order that is mythological rather than historical. One myth replaces another. One has only to read Heidegger to appreciate his linguistic, idiosyncratic meanings and the new words he had to create to express his philosophy. These words did not enter the language of common speech and meaning, but they did create a space for those who read him to see the world differently. He created a discourse that brought new words into the languages into which his work was translated.

Ricoeur tells us that the act of creating a new discourse is an event set in time and space and in a social setting. One can talk about the *event-ful-ness* of postmodernist experimentation. The postmodernist seeks is to make language self-reflective or related to its own inner code, wrestled from accepted social norms.

In a created discourse, myth attacks history and the order of personal irrationality attacks the order of social rationality. Such discourse is subversive and the social implications of that action result in its being attacked by the populist voice as elitist. "Give us back our ordinary meanings and our tried and true myths" cry the unnerved populists as they condemn the postmodernist voice. For them it is elitist gibberish and useless experimentation, irrelevant to the real world in which the populace lives and works.

The basic division in this debate is between those for whom the text is subordinate to its role as social glue and those for whom the text is self-sufficient and self-expressive, allowing the author the freedom of individuality. In postmodernism, language is configured in an anti-linear way as part of the project of linguistic self-reference in which words are more important than what they refer to. Postmodern language seems to go round and round in its own preoccupations. This circularity is designed to "unbuild" the culturally sanctioned meanings of words because those old meanings are insufficient to describe the world. This "opening up" is necessary work. In Kroetsch's poetry the linguistic conventions of English are looked upon as too linear and simple. The language is re-spaced and broken up like a farmer rearranging a field. For van Herk's novels English is too patriarchal in its roots and needs to be upset by a challenging female voice. For Kostash English is too English and must be ethnicized, while for Wah it is too white and Eurocentric. There is a sense of grievance against English because it is imperial at its source and speaks assimilation rather than diversity.

The post-structuralist philosopher Jacques Derrida claimed that there is nothing but text and language to mould our understanding. This interpretation of reality as a linguistic/cultural construct that needs constant reconstruction appeals to writers because it gives them power over reality. Or does it? Each of these writers rebels against the canon, but their authenticity depends on their having that very canon within them. Theirs is the language of self-transformation not social transformation. It is a personal therapy that gives them the sense of individual creativity. But literary originality requires more than just a beginning. The beginning only exists as a beginning when a middle and an end appear, and these literary liberators have not established a language for others whose goal is social liberation, a new language for the masses. Their work may be recognized for being different and accomplished but not for being a new voice of the populace. The literary avant-garde is rightly heralded by its own cadres (people like myself), but its influence does not penetrate the great subconscious. Nor does its literary influence extend beyond the region, imprinting its linguistic innovations upon others. The project to create a literary breakthrough in the historical reality of Western Canada has resulted in individual solutions rather than collective ones, making the language of postmodernism in Western Canada the language of the self.

As the literary avant-garde in a hinterland region working in an imperial system, these four writers have ended up bringing the world and its literary concerns to the region rather than exporting a new way of looking at the world. They seek to be contemporary and expressive of what is most of interest using local materials, but the leap from that stance to one in which their writing generates imitation has not occurred. Is asking this asking too much? Yes, it is too much when the originating or founding power is missing. Western Canadian literature has been an imported sensibility and continues to be a conduit for world-historical forces rather than a world-historical force itself. The regional persists, absorbing the universal into its particularity, acting like a reflective moon rather than an explosive sun.

Two American futurists described the postmodernist universe that we live in as a paradigm shift from a culture in which standards are clearly defined and hierarchical to one in which individuals must pluck elements from a rotating maelstrom to form their own individual mosaic or collage of meaning.[6] This is precisely what these Western Canadian writers have done. In seeking to find their own voices they have rejected traditional meanings and sought to create new ones, but those meanings have not become established in the wider society as a genuine expression of its collective aspirations, nor have they made either a national or international impact in terms of eager followers and imitators, a sign of originality.

These are writers who have inherited a tradition that is imported and externally generated. Writing out of here means embracing a fundamental alienation, a certain inherent strangeness that cannot be escaped. All English narration about this place, even when it is written here, is also from elsewhere, carrying in its cultural and historical baggage trends and styles that do not originate here. It is as if the project of originality can only occur when the imperial legacy is somehow overcome, and that overcoming cannot come through literary style alone but through political and social change in which the dominant meta-narrative is replaced with a new story created by the people as a whole.

The postmodernist writers of the West have articulated the regional project as the struggle for social equality for their identity politics and liberation from inherited cultural forms. But that project is rooted in the postmodernist and postcolonialist project that they have inherited from outside the region. They have adapted it to their individual issues and concerns and they have expressed its desire for change in their writing. The work that has resulted from this adaptation has been important for the literary elite, but has had little, if any, impact on the wider regional society. The very intellectualism of this project has kept it consciously outside the populist norms of ordinary writing and language.

So what about the yellowed sheets from the 1980 lectures at the University of Lethbridge on prairie writing? Are they just so much old paper and old ideas? Not quite. They recognized the feminism of van Herk, the issue of white males writing about aboriginal cultures, the struggle against Anglo tradition as a dominant monoculture, and the importance of the symbolic in rectifying historical injustices, but they did not realize that post-modernism was the term that would describe the new era of Western Canadian writing that came to dominate the 1990s. Its creation and celebration of multiple competing narratives must be acknowledged, but likewise we need to admit that the postmodernist moment in regional writing has not produced a writing that influenced work outside the region and that the region's writing remains dependent on influences from outside. The role of Western Canadian writing as an adapter of global literary trends continues.

I Am Butler:

Notes for an Autobiographical Long Poem

WHILE WRITING THE FIRST VOLUME OF THE *Literary History of Alberta* I became fascinated with the personality of William Francis Butler, a British military officer who was stationed in Canada for a brief period. He made three journeys to the Canadian West in 1870, 1872 and 1883, each of which he described in a book. *The Great Lone Land* was published in 1872 to great interest and described his experiences with the insurrectionary leader Louis Riel and his later travel to scout out the Blackfoot Confederacy in what is now southern Alberta. *The Wild North Land* was published in 1873 as a kind of autobiographical sequel. It described Butler's self-financed winter journey to the northern reaches of the region ending in British Columbia and the Pacific coast. His 1883 trip to the Canadian West is briefly described in his posthumously published autobiography, *Sir William Butler* (1911).

What drew me to Butler? It was his writing. *The Great Lone Land* is a classic work of Victorian travel and exploration literature and an important volume in the literary history of the region. In spite of a very active military career, Butler ended up writing twenty books including biographies and a volume of popular juvenile fiction. Quite simply he was a fine writer. Then there was his involvement in the Riel Rebellion, a seminal event in the evolution of the Western Canadian identity, which led to the birth of the province of Manitoba. At one point I imagined I would write a new biography of the man with an emphasis on his writing. The one and only biography had been published in 1967 by the eminent Western Canadian literary critic and novelist Edward McCourt, who was, like Butler, Irish. I was attracted to Butler because of my regionalism, my own work as a non-fiction writer, and my view of him as an anti-establishment outsider, an identity forced on him by his ethnic Irish background. But in the end I realized that what I wanted to say about Butler would best be said in a poem, a long poem.

The venerable Canadian poet Phyllis Webb, in an essay titled "Poetry and Psychobiography," warned that "poetic knowing is always in advance of the poet."[7] What is this poetic knowing she refers to? When I write a long poem about Butler using the voice of the "I," then I am really using two "I's"—his autobiographical first person and my own first person in which I combine the knowledge he presents in his non-fiction with the knowing I present in the poem. As the writer of the long poem I become an actor who impersonates a character, creating a different character for the reader than the one Butler created of himself. When an actor does a Mark Twain monologue on a stage, the audience is drawn into the fantasy that it is Mark Twain it is viewing and listening to. It is no different in an autobiographical poem not written by the original self. I ask myself, Is the poem more me than him? Surely the poem as a work of art will be mine more than his and yet the words will convey an autobiographical conceit—that he is the one speaking and not I. The meaning of the poem will lie in its fundamental act of hiding this truth, so that the words conceal the author behind the facade of Butler's first-person singular.

A late-twentieth-century narrative is radically different from a late-nineteenth-century narrative. I may live in the same geographic area in which he travelled but I dwell in a cultural universe that he could not imagine. And yet I read his narratives, enjoy them and criticize them because I can see something familiar in them. What is really going on is a kind of dialogue. The past writer is read by the present writer who then creates writing about that past writer as he imagines him to have been. This is a complicated and dangerous process. The search for truth can be a great cover for many disguises. If Butler had also described his journeys in a long poem, which would be more truthful—the poem or the non-fiction account?

How does this dialogue combine narratives? Seek commonality? What does the voice of a Victorian imperial writer have to do with an ethnic Western Canadian more than a century later? Whose story is really being told in the poem? What are the rules of impersonation? These questions run through my mind and lead to only more questions, as long as the poem remains unwritten. The poem is a literary journey similar to Butler's physical journey. It begins at a certain place, at a certain time, and it ends, like every journey. The text began in 1997 but situates itself in 1870. It may be written in or outside the region and it will pretend that it is a document from the past. In the process of becoming a narrative the internal worlds of two men—the contemporary poet and the historical man he is impersonating combine into a single "I." The poet seeks to create an invisible seam linking two histories, two personalities and radically different narratives into a single reality called a long poem. The poet creates a fictional autobiography, but he also creates history and biography. He is rewriting the past.

My identification with Butler is the crucial beginning of the journey. I was the one who felt that he was essentially an outsider, based on the information he provided in his autobiography. Since I ascribe the category of "outsider" to myself, I end up centralizing it in my understanding of Butler. It is the empathetic key that I need to begin the work. Second, I have within me a deep suspicion, after reading both Butler's autobiography and McCourt's biography, that there is so much hidden about Butler in both narratives that the public face that Butler was so good at drawing was a magnificent mask used for public consumption. As a biographer of others and the author of volumes about himself and his exploits, Butler was an expert in giving people what they wanted. He was loyal to his readership and to his public persona. In distrusting Butler's narrative of nobility I was seeking a more realistic Butler based on my own perspective.

I wanted to test myself. For years I had been an essayist and historian, a non-fiction writer about the West. I had only recently published my first book of poems. They were short lyrical poems and I wanted to see if I could go further by writing a long poem about an important figure—a single poem filling a whole volume. Butler's Western travels fit the bill. Could I match in poetry what Butler had achieved in his prose? Did I have the endurance? The commitment? The confidence? Could I accomplish a long literary march and come out the other side with a better knowledge of Butler, the region and myself? That was my Butler-like test. The poem fit both our personalities.

To explore what I was bringing to Butler's autobiographical self as a persona in my poem I began by examining two topics of interest to both of us—first, an important figure that Butler describes and second, the Western landscape. Riel, the great revolutionary Western Canadian leader, who led two insurrections against the Canadian government in the nineteenth century and was eventually hanged, is that important figure. His death turned him into a great Canadian myth and symbol, but for Butler he was flesh and blood. In *The Great Lone Land*, Butler describes his 1870 meeting with Louis Riel in this way:

> He was dressed in a curious mixture of clothing—a black frock-coat, vest and trousers; but the effect of this somewhat clerical costume was not a little marred by a pair of Indian moccasins, which nowhere look more out of place than on a carpeted floor.[8]

Butler goes on to report that after shaking hands with Riel he continued the game of billiards he had been playing, thereby unnerving the President of the Provisional Government. There is one aspect of this description that caught my attention—the out-of-placeness of the moccasins. Butler made much of this in his account, emphasizing the backwoods character of Riel as a frontiersman. No doubt, Lieutenant Butler was wearing civilized leather boots, in his mind and that of his British readers a far superior product. I do not doubt Butler's description, though I have yet to see a photograph of Riel in moccasins. But I have seen a photo from the second Riel Rebellion of the members of the 1885 Provisional Government under arrest, most of whom are in frock coats and moccasins.

The moccasins are a basic expression of the Metis identity that Riel represented. Butler was aware of this. So am I. Contemporary Western Canadian culture is also aware of this crucial artifact and its political implications. Winnipeg, then named Fort Garry, where the events Butler describes took place, has a statue to Riel situated on the banks of the Red River by the Legislative grounds. This new statue was erected to replace a statue first put

UPPER FORT GARRY, RED RIVER SETTLEMENT.

UPPER FORT GARRY

For the reader of the Illustrated London News, *the fort epitomized the stability and security of the English castle and the necessity of its retrieval from the rebels. Illustration:* Illustrated London News, *February 12, 1870, p. 169.*

up in 1970 to celebrate the centennial of Manitoba and Riel as its father because he had fought to have the Northwest admitted to Canada as an equal province of Confederation. The older statue showed a naked, twisted human figure, a symbolic expression of the agonizing birth of the province. The new statue, favoured by the Metis Association of Manitoba, presents a dignified, states-manlike Riel in a frock coat and moccasins. Did the sculptor read Butler? I don't know, but I do know that the moccasins were not at all out of place in 1870 when Butler met him but were very much an expression of indigenous reality and political vision. I suspect Butler sensed this, because he was an acute observer, and so he made sure he made light of it in order to maintain his impe-rial superiority.

In the poem this scene becomes a battleground for my vision of Riel and his place in my mythological universe compared to Butler's first-hand, imperially politicized vision. Butler painted Riel as an outsider, while I will paint Butler as the outsider and Riel as the insider. This reversal is tricky since the autobiographi-cal format demands that this idea of mine be conveyed in Butler's imagined voice—a voice I will create inside his mind rather than the voice Butler himself projected on the published page. I have already written about these moccasins in a poem published in *Ribstones* and titled "Riel." The last stanza reads:

> *we have come*
> *for a miracle*
> *that does not happen.*
> *Your moccasins*
> *have turned to bronze.*[9]

The bronze reality of the statue has replaced the soft moose-hide moccasins that were part of the living Riel. They symbolize an idealized Riel mythologized into an icon that is sacred and untouchable. In mythology bronze triumphs over flesh. In poetry flesh must return and triumph over history. The baby that has its first shoes bronzed grows into an adult, and then the adoring parents, having lived through childhood and teenagehood, look back on those bronzed booties as artifacts of an idealized time. That is why the statue must become part of the poem—because of its bronze moccasins à la Butler.

A second issue the poem will deal with is Butler's affinity for the Western landscape. In his second book of travels, *The Wild North Land,* Butler provides an eloquent description of the prairie region as an epic landscape so beloved by Victorian sensibility:

> *He who rides for months through the vast solitudes sees during the hours of his daily travel an unbroken panorama of distance. The seasons come and go; grass grows and flowers die; the fire leaps with tiger bounds along the earth; the snow lies still and quiet over hill and lake; the rivers rise and fall, but the rigid features of the wilderness rest unchanged...the weight of the Infinite seems to brood over it. Once only in the hours of day and night a moment comes when this impassive veil is drawn...the moment which follows the sunset...In a deep sea of emerald and orange of fifty shades, mingled and interwoven together, rose-coloured isles float anchored to great golden threads...the parting sun's last gift, reddens upwards to the zenith.*[10]

This is fairly typical of Butler's grandiloquent style and it raises a key metaphor for the Western Canadian identity, that of the figure in the landscape. Here is Butler the solitary rider, a romantic figure on horseback set against a magnificently empty landscape equated with the passage of the sun, which is the only mobile element in the vast terrain. The image of the figure in the landscape was explored by the Western Canadian literary critic Lawrence Ricou in *Vertical Man / Horizontal World* (1973). Ricou wrote that the essential prairie literary image is of a human's "curiously abrupt position in a vast and uninterrupted landscape."[11] The solitude of the landscape is the context that emphasized the solitariness of the figure in that landscape. Butler's picturesque expression of the Western Canadian landscape may be bound by Victorian convention but it is nevertheless basic to regional understanding. I too have seen such sunsets on the prairie, those self-same purple islands of clouds floating on the glowing horizon, especially in summer when the days are long, the nights short. In the poem Butler and I will compare sunsets.

The importance of the sunset image to prairie identity is confirmed in Butler's 1911 autobiography in which he described his disillusioning journey of 1883. He was particularly upset by the decline of the First Nations peoples since the last time he had been in the West a decade earlier. He found post-treaty life on reserves pitiful and his romantic noble savage no more. He writes:

> *One thing was still here unchanged: it was the twilight. Before that hour came the stage had reached its stopping place, and I was able to get away from its atmosphere to some neighbouring hill, or by the edge of some lakelet, where one could look again at some of the old sights, the great red sun going slowly down over the immense landscape, and leaving the western sky a vast half dome of rose-tipped wavelets from horizon to zenith.*[12]

The great red setting sun was, of course, his metaphor for the decline of the aboriginal people in the post-buffalo period and the end of the frontier. The twilight of the red man was a piety of late-nineteenth-century Victorian thought and Butler expressed it with the right mix of inevitability, nostalgia and pity.

THE PRAIRIE CREES.

THE PRAIRIE CREE

*In this engraving of the Cree as imagined by the artist,
the English reader sees an anomolous, but familiar, English riding saddle.
Illustration: Illustrated London News, June 4, 1870, p. 569*

Butler was, like all of us, a walking contradiction. While sympa-
thizing with their former greatness, Butler was an agent of their
demise both in 1870 and again in 1883, when he was on a mission
for a land settlement consortium in Britain that hoped to purchase a vast tract of land for pioneer settlement.

Butler's attraction to the aboriginal world (but not its Metis
manifestation) has also been my attraction as a Western Canadian
living in a region with a continuing significant aboriginal presence. History hasn't wiped out the native power and it still resides
in Western Canada. The first book I published, in 1977, was a collection of essays by the Metis architect Douglas Cardinal, the
designer of the Museum of Civilization in Ottawa and the
Museum of the American Indian in Washington, D.C. A later
book of mine contained essays such as "The Metis Metaphor" and
"Toward an Indigenous Society," which were indicative of my
interest.[13] Like Butler I have turned to the First Nations peoples
of Western Canada for an understanding of the region and, like
him, I have used my own idiom to express that understanding. In
the poem, I intend to provide the aboriginal voice with its own
persona, which will be complicated since that persona will speak
to Butler in his dreams as he lies under the prairie stars, mutter-
ing to himself. The thought has crossed my mind that I may even
have Geronimo appear in his dream in the guise of a Saharan
Dervish, a symbol of all the native leaders that Butler fought from
North America to Africa. Their most important discussion will
centre on the colour red.

In his biography *Remember Butler,* Edward McCourt recounts
how Butler received a message from Theodore Roosevelt in 1910.
Butler was dying and the ex-President's expression of admiration
for *The Great Lone Land* cheered him up.[14] The book went through
numerous printings and editions and so became its own kind of

icon. In a sense Butler became a major figure in the landscape of the West but more as a writer than as a soldier. We visualize him standing up, pen in hand, soaking in the farflung horizon and creating an image that excited thousands upon thousands of readers. But the poem will capture him outside that noble public stance that he gave himself and will, instead, see him lying down, with the horizontal existence of an ordinary mortal rather than the vertical existence reserved for a heroic figure. Butler made himself by writing about his deeds; I hope to unmake Butler by writing about his imagined private thoughts.

The task of the long autobiographical poem is to give us a previously unknown Butler, a story we haven't heard before, either from Butler or from others. A more truthful Butler? Perhaps. Perhaps not. Phyllis Webb helps me understand the journey I've embarked on. "Narratizing is an aspect of consciousness itself," she writes, attributing the concept to Julian Jaynes. "We narratize our own lives from minute to minute; we narratize sensory experience into shapely clusters or gestalts, to make sense, and making sense means structurally making story."[15] My narrative is not Butler's but my own and when I narratize or fictionalize him I am also narrating my own life and values and beliefs. I am making my sense not his, while I pretend that it is his sense, not mine.

Postmodernism is the philosophy of literature that helps best understand the dimensions of this game that I am playing. Robert Kroetsch, the Western Canadian novelist and poet, and partisan of postmodernist understanding, is the one who resurrected the Western Canadian long poem in the 1970s. What better person could there be but Kroetsch to guide me in the right direction? In an article subtitled "Robert Kroetsch Rewriting the Great Plains," Francis Kaye and Robert Thacker raise the issue of how regionalism and postmodernism can co-exist and they turn to Kroetsch for the answer. He is the alchemist par excellence who has made this unlikely marriage happen. They write about post-modernism's "search for the hidden" and how the past is always concealed by the present because narratives "are partly invented and partly discovered."[16] This is precisely what this long poem is all about—the search for the self-concealed Butler, who is brought forth through the postmodernist prism of my present, using dis-covery and invention. Kroetsch has already done this superbly in his novels and poems, creating a past that is more truthful than historical writing.

In an essay titled "On Being an Alberta Writer," which Kroetsch wrote some years ago, the eminent writer tells us that "The great sub-text of prairie literature is our oral tradition."[17] The poem and the song are the greatest examples of the oral tradition, of the spoken word in all its rhetorical splendour. It is Butler's oral tradition that the poem seeks to create, a voice that is not written down. It seeks out his innermost thoughts, whether spoken or unspoken, but always unwritten, and returns them to the world. The words of the poem will contain many of Butler's words as I imagine them to be, but none of his written words because the already written words would betray my inventing and discovering role. His words have done their act of hiding and now my words have to do theirs.

Kroetsch has also written, "Resisting history, we take on the burden of a concealed history. Claiming to remember, we discover the slippage that transforms memory into history and fiction alike."[18] McCourt titled his book on Butler *Remember Butler*, as if to say that he had been forgotten and deserved to be remembered. The memories that McCourt put forward as a biographer were generally those of Butler himself. As a poet I can resist history, as Kroetsch advises, thereby taking on the burden of Butler's concealment, and rather than exposing it the way a biographer might, I seek only to rewrite it as a new concealment.

Kroetsch trusts the truth of fiction over the truth of non-fiction. This choice of truths is what allows the actor to act and the poet to write. One is not bound by documentary evidence because the document itself is distrusted. One writer on post-modernism has described it as thought based on "a loss of belief in an objective world and an incredulity towards metanarratives of legitimation...there is no foundation to secure a universal and objective reality."[19] The poem replaces the so-called objectivity of the autobiographical account presented in Butler's books with the subjectivity of the autobiographical poem in which the subconscious is more important than the conscious and the interpretation of the meaning between the lines more important than the text itself.

"I Am Butler" creates a poetic reality that is based on a sub-version of Butler's texts that leads to a certain kind of truth or knowing particular to the poetic form. A new myth is born in the long poem just as a new Mark Twain is born in the performance of an actor pretending to be him. The poem gives us a new William Francis Butler as imagined by the poet and not by Butler himself. Canada's great analyst of postmodernism, Linda Hutcheon, has pointed out the importance of ideology in postmodernist understanding. The postmodernist, to use her words, creates "a system of meanings operating within certain codes and conventions that are socially produced and historically conditioned. This is the postmodern focus that has replaced the modernist/romantic one of individual expression."[20] My meanings are not Butler's. His world is not mine. We share a geographic space but our cultures are radically different. I am remaking him in my own image, just as he remade himself in the image valued by his time. So the

Butler poem becomes an anti-Butler poem. It seeks to demythol-
ogize and then remythologize, expressing the view that what is
important about a human life is the unspoken, the subterranean
self that we keep hidden as best we can, but Butler's inner self is
my creation, my understanding and my imagining.

If the literary Butler is the romantic and heroic figure of the
individual beloved by the late Victorians, then the postmodernist
poet is the epitome of self-conscious ideological correctness in
the late twentieth century. The resulting poem creates a postmodernist Butler who can only exist in the imagination of the
poet and in the conventions of his day. Is this an affront to the so-
called real Butler? I don't think so. Butler was perfectly self-conscious of the rules and limitations of his literary universe. He
would understand the game I'm playing because he played it
himself. If my world wants and can only digest a postmodernist
Butler, then that is the Butler I will give it. The subterranean
Butler I want to bring to the surface in the poem is what my
world expects and I must fulfill its expectations. There is no quest
for certainty here, no claim to historical truth or validity. In fact,
I want to create Butler as he might be if he lived in our own time,
made in our own image. Butler is lifted from the restrictions of
history and mortality and becomes a god-hero resurrected
through the regenerative power of myth.

When I look at Butler and create a persona for him based
on discovery and invention, I am simply creating a new disguise
for him, one that he has never had before. This is my art and the
very heart of the matter. The American Jungian writer James
Hillman recently published a best-selling book, *The Soul's Code,*
in which he praises disguises, especially those created by writers.
"Autobiography is itself essentially duplicitous" he tells us.[21] But
it is right to be that way. "The fables I tell," he goes on to say, "more

truly tell who I am."[22] That fable-quality of the autobiographical poem actually tells more about the poet than any truth-claims. What did not happen or is imagined to have happened may help us understand and know Butler better than a litany of facts about his life. At least, we will know him as we know others around us rather than as he knew himself. He will be less of a stranger to us in the poem than in his own century-old texts because we are not part of his world and cannot really grasp it from the inside. So what the poem seeks to achieve is the remaking of Butler from his present-day status as a man outside our culture into a present-day insider, which he was in his own day as a writer.

Sharon Butala is Western Canada's leading contemporary writer on nature and spirituality. In her autobiographical book, *The Perfection of the Morning: An Apprenticeship in Nature* (1994), she tells us that her "sense of alienation and being alone in the world" found salvation "in the wash of golden light" at the end of a day on the prairie landscape.[23] Butler's sublime world is also Butala's sublime world, where "all desire for heaven is absorbed in the glowing, fragile plains, the radiant hills."[24] Butala lives on a ranch near the Cypress Hills in southwestern Saskatchewan, not far from the world of Wallace Stegner's *Wolf Willow*. She lives in the heart of Butler's *Great Lone Land* and though she sees with the eyes of a late-twentieth-century woman, his sunsets are also her sunsets. Perhaps she too will appear in the poem bringing a womanly sensibility to Butler's universe, a sensibility he ignored throughout his writings.

My thoughts on the Butler poem are coming to a close, but there are two things that I envision as being essential to the long poem—the first is illustration or picture and the second is mirror. Several years ago my mother-in-law, Virginia Berry, a prominent historian of Manitoba art, offered me a choice of historic illustrations from a show that she had organized some years ago at the Winnipeg Art Gallery. I selected illustrations from the *Illustrated London News* and *Picturesque Canada* that would suit the Butler book. I felt that the poem could not speak properly without these Victorian illustrations counterbalancing my own postmodernist voice. If a picture is worth a thousand words then surely these pictures would say more to the readers than the poem. They would serve as substitutes for Butler's verbal pictures since the illustrators would have used texts like Butler's to create their imaginary images of the West.

The second presence in the poem is a mirror. It is the mirror that I believe Butler carried with him in his travelling case to remind him of who he was and his place in the great imperial British universe. It is a mirror that displays not only his face but also his clothes. His costume and the mirror will exist not only in my narrative but also in the form of photographs of Butler displaying himself in all his finery. These formal Victorian photographs are full of pose and presentation. Their pomp is a cultural artifact that confirms my search for the person underneath the uniform. They are so rigid and unnatural that they cry out for a more human representation, which is what I hope the readers will find in the poem. When I finally saw a photograph of Butler crouching beside the husky dog he had on his 1872 winter trip, I was shocked. He was dressed in a frontier-style bowler hat and civilian clothes. He didn't fit the military image I had of him based on his official photos and the voice of his narrative, which conveyed authority and mission. He looked like an American carpetbagger rather than a red coat. If one photo can be so devastating when put up against the series of formal military portraits placed in his autobiography, then how much more revealing could a poem be that seeks to strip the author of his artificial, protective shell?

As a mirror, the postmodernist autobiographical poem shows a reflection, a reflection not of Butler, but of the poet disguised as and disguising Butler. In Butler's mirror I see myself though I try to hide that self from others. The object in the mirror/photographs is the subject of the poem and as a subject it becomes automatically an object. The real subject, the poet, is meant to disappear in the flash of a magician's smoke, leaving us with Butler stripped of his uniform and lying down, reflecting on how he idealized reality and how now reality is seeking its vengeance. McCourt described William Francis Butler as "a soldier of great distinction, a traveller in wild and lonely places; and among soldier-travellers the best writer of them all."[25] His poet will ignore his distinction and call him a common spy, excise the solitude with ghosts and seek to write him as he would write himself today, a man exposed rather than imposed.

Postscript: *Fellow writers have warned me not to write this paper because in writing it, they say, I will say everything I have in me on the topic and so will never write the poem. But I could not resist the temptation to write a kind of critique of the poem before the poem was even written. What could be more postmodernist? Perhaps their prophecy will be Butler's non-fiction revenge on my poetic self, the autobiographer having the last laugh on his pseudo-biographer.*

SIR WILLIAM F. BUTLER

Photo: National Archives of Canada / C-021287.

Identity and
the Western Writer:
Literary Objects
and Literary Saints

WHEN I WAS A BOY GROWING UP IN WINNIPEG, my older cousin Irene let me have three books that had belonged to her from the years we had all spent in Germany after the War. The first book was an English-German dictionary, a cheaply produced paperback published in Munich in 1946, the year I was born. She had used it as a student, living in the American-occupied zone of southern Germany, where our family were refugees. The second book was also a dictionary, but this time it was an English-Ukrainian dictionary, again with a cheap brown paper cover, and published by a Ukrainian language co-operative set up after the war in Germany. The third book was smaller than the other two. It was the second volume of the poetry of Ukraine's poet laureate, Taras Shevchenko. It was also a poor-quality paperback just like the others. On the inside there was a reproduction of the poet's image and on the title page at the bottom there were two words indicating where the book was published—*na chuzini,* meaning "abroad," "foreign land" or "in exile." Although the book was in Ukrainian, the verso side of the title page carried an English-language inscription that

read PERMITTED BY AUTHORITY OF THE MILITARY GOV-
ERNMENT.

I have kept these three tattered and decrepit books since my
youth and I revere them because of the meaning they carry for
me. They represent my roots in a tripartite identity—the son of a
refugee Ukrainian family, born in Germany after the war, and
destined to make his home in Western Canada and become a
writer in the English language. As books they symbolize my career
as a writer. As dictionaries they point to the multilingual universe
I inhabit. The book of poetry signals my writerly attachment to
the poetic form. But these books are more than just visual metaphors of my life. They are signs of my life project—my trajectory.
They have identified me as a writer living within a space delineat-
ed by three things—translation, poetry and authority.

When I think of identity I think of something that is inter-
nally generated rather than an image that is generated externally.
Identity is that side of ourselves that we create, while image is that
side of us created by others. An example of how identity and
image are opposites is evident in the debate over Quebec independence. Those who seek independence for Quebec call themselves sovereigntists, which they view as a positive term because it
suggests building a new country, while those who attack Quebec
independence call those same people separatists, a negative term
suggesting destruction. The identity I am referring to is not the
image you may or may not have of me, but an identity generated
within my own being. To say that I am a non-fiction writer, an
essayist, a poet, a historian is true but it doesn't tell you very
much about George Melnyk and the way I understand myself.

The word "identity" is rooted in the Latin word *idem,*
which means "the same," as in the word "identical." Identity
means a self that continues with a certain sameness. There is both

THE DICTIONARY

One of the three books given to George by his cousin Irene.

a sense of permanence in having an identity and a sense of being identified with something or someone or some place. Through identity and identification what is inside me is also outside me. What I identify with and who I identify with are two basic aspects of a self-generated identity.

When I think of identity as it relates to my being a writer I think immediately of those three aspects bequeathed to me by the books I've mentioned—my identity as an act of translation, as an act of poetry and as an act of authority. Let me begin with the first—translation. Having been raised in a Western Canadian world in which my first language, which is Ukrainian, is considered "alien" or "foreign," I have fulfilled the prophecy in the second volume of Taras Shevchenko's poetry that appeared on the title page as *na chuzini*. I live on foreign soil. I exist in a language that is foreign, which the dictionaries also indicated was to be my fate. Even though I have fought desperately to be completely of this place, its language and its regional identity, I can never escape foreignness. I am after all an immigrant. Even though this English-speaking world of Western Canada is my world, my home and my literary identity, I know that there are so many dimensions to that identity that involve translation, the essence of foreignness. This should not be surprising since expressing the identical is the basis of all dictionaries that seek to equate words from different languages. Throughout my literary life I have taken the cultural and religious images of my Ukrainian upbringing and expressed those images in the cultural and religious images of Western Canada. For example, I have always equated my being taught about Ukraine's struggle for independence with my own later concern for Western regional autonomy.

Every Western Canadian writer whose world begins in another place, whether inside or outside Canada, is involved in acts of translation, of moving images from one world into another and trying to establish some sort of equation between them the way a dictionary does. We develop metaphors for our lives, interpret ourselves through ideas that come from other places and other realities, and give ourselves an identity that does not match what people may see on the surface. We create our own symbols from objects that are dear to us, like the three books that are dear to me, and from stories and events that we put together in the creation of our own idiosyncratic mythology about ourselves, which often remains a personal secret. As writers we end up being translators of our own lives.

The second aspect of identity bequeathed to me by those books is the act of poetry. Obviously not all writers write or publish poetry, yet all Western Canadian writers engage in acts of poetry. By poetry I mean our stance before the world expressed in the Greek term *poesis*, a way of being in the world that allows us to be overwhelmed by it as we stand in awe. No matter how prosaic our writing or how mechanical or formulaic our approach is, there is always a spark of *poesis* in our words that represents the self, that inner identity that we carry within us subconsciously. For the Greeks, *poesis* resulted in the creation of metaphor, and every writer, poet, novelist and journalist creates metaphors, which are similarities or equivalencies that ring true in the mind of the reader even if that writer does not use what are considered grammatical constructs called metaphors. We always write in a metaphoric way, building associations for ourselves and our readers. What poetry does is add to the wealth of symbols and mythology that our acts of translation first establish by giving the world a metaphoric, structured meaning in which we can place ourselves. Poetry is the doll house in which we play. Another way of thinking of the poetic (metaphoric) nature of identity is the mythology in family stories and the wider culture. These metaphors become the internal interpreters of our lives and the lives of others. We see the world and ourselves through them. We literally breathe the meaning that these metaphors give and we exhale them into the world. Without them we could not exist as writers or as people.

The third aspect of identity is authority—the authorization that we create by virtue of our being authors. The great psychologist Carl Jung tells us that truth is superior to authority, thereby suggesting that there is contradiction between the truth writers try to express and the authority inherent in their authorship. The authorization of the military censor concerning Shevchenko's poetry is totally insignificant compared to the vast authority of both the poetry itself and the legendary quality Ukrainian culture has built around it. And yet that insignificant censor's external authority was necessary to allow the poetry to exist in that book form. Of course, authority and author come from the same root. In authorizing, the censor was not writing but condoning this written text. He was approving its creation and allowing its existence. Was this unknown person the one who authorized my authorial voice?

The truth of a people authorizes its legitimacy, but when that truth exists in a foreign land it requires a foreign authority to legitimize it. Because of this process, an outsider's *poesis* can be hidden from the eyes of the dominant power lest it be misinterpreted as a threat, the way foreignness often is. Knowing what to say in a foreign land only adds complexity to the games that truth and authority play with each other.

Jung is saying that there is an inner truth that comes from within the self, based on our personal subconscious and on the collective subconscious, which is in conflict with the external

NA CHUZINI

The image of Taras Shevchenko faces the title page of his second volume of poetry. The bottom left of the title page reads na chuzini—*"published in exile." Why does the book have a V-cut in it? A mystery.*

images created for us by society and its acts of censorship and repression. I had no idea when I was a teenager that my accepting these three books would point to my being involved in a lifelong struggle against censorship, first as a broadcast journalist and then as a writer. But that is what happened. The censor has always been with me, and the authority of the author, as represented by Shevchenko's poetry, has been in conflict with the wider society and its agents. After twenty-five years in Alberta I remain a literary dissident, opposed to the official ideology of the state. And it seems that the fight against government censorship in Alberta never ends. It is a permanent battle that only intensifies with time.

But Jung's view of truth and authority is deeper than this simple internal-external dichotomy. He is actually getting at the dual nature of all authority and truth even when it is our inner truth and authority as authors that are involved. All truth-claims are suspect as authority because of their utter subjectivity and because society's definition of truth is so totally and nihilistically objective, stripping truth of any and all subjectivity. In society's view of truth there is no subjectivity, while in self-centred truth, objectivity is an enemy. Neither the individual's truth nor the truth offered by society is complete. Authority and truth, Jung tells us, are two warring sides of the coin that is language, just as image and identity are two warring sides of the self. The authority we claim for ourselves as writers based on some internal truth ends up being suspect because, using Jung's paradigm, truth is only a half-truth. It is a half-truth because what we *author-ize* in our writing is based as much on what we hide as what we reveal. I have found that throughout my writing life I have created my authority as an author through this repressive mechanism of concealment. This concealment has been necessary in order to continue "revealing." Without that vast reservoir of hiddenness my revelation of truth would stop and with it all my *author-ity*. In other words, that military censor continues to live within me and will as long as I write. He lives not only within me but within all writers.

The intermingling of translation, poetry and authority is the "what" of my identity, but the "who" of my identity involves the figure of a literary hero like Shevchenko. Yet an incident from my childhood in Winnipeg illustrates how my identification with Shevchenko resulted in a retreat from the Ukrainian language. As a young boy I was scheduled to perform a very famous poem by Shevchenko at a celebration at our church. My mother dressed me up in a white shirt and bow tie. I had memorized the poem in perfect Ukrainian, but when I got up to recite it I froze. I just couldn't say a word. My mind was blank. Eventually I left the stage humiliated and an embarrassment to my family, which resulted in my having a stutter that took years to overcome. I now interpret this incident as a sign that Ukrainian was not to be the language of my poetry and of my writing. I gave up on Shevchenko and in a symbolic way I gave up my maternal tongue. When I lost Shevchenko as a literary hero, I had to find a replacement that somehow reflected his spirit in my new language— English. I found that hero in Andrew Suknaski, one of Saskatchewan's greatest poets. On the wall of my study there is a black and white woodcut that I did of him twenty years ago, when he was at the height of his poetic power. It is a simple silhouette of Andy with his balding head and thick moustache as he smokes his trademark pipe. When I carved this image I was conscious of equating Andrew Suknaski, the suffering poet, with Taras Shevchenko, the long-suffering exiled poet of Ukraine. It was a conscious translation made easier because Andy was also of Ukrainian descent. In my mind he became a Western Canadian equivalent of Shevchenko. The sad and tragic expression that I put in Suknaski's face is the sensibility I associated with all the images of Shevchenko that have come down to us.

My first book of poetry, *Ribstones*, contained a poem I wrote about Andy Suknaski titled "The Poet." That poem best expresses all the conflicts between truth and authority that is part of every writer's identity. It was also the literary equivalent of the woodcut that I had made.

> *I have read*
> *that he smashes poems*
> *with his fists,*
> *blood bursts*
> *from his eyes,*
> *words grind*
> *out of his teeth.*
>
> *I have seen*
> *the bare corner of his basement room,*
> *two small windows held*
> *shut by nails, the bed,*
> *steel chair, frying pan, fridge*
> *and poems hung*
> *from metal hanger.*
>
> *He fears broken futures,*
> *the wandering of soul,*
> *alcoholic joy,*
> *being beaten up*
> *by dreams, old myths,*
> *fantasy.*[26]

The poem has come true. Today, Andy's soul is wandering, his future seems broken, he has suffered from alcoholic joy, he has been beaten up by dreams, myths and his own fantasies. He lives in a group home in Moose Jaw. He no longer creates. There are resonances of Shevchenko's Siberian exile in the poem—where did Shevchenko hang his illegal poems? What small basement room did he inhabit? I don't know but I can imagine that the parallels between Shevchenko and Suknaski are many.

The identity of a writer is a terribly complex thing to unravel and even when we succeed in pinpointing little bits and pieces, various connections here and there, we always seem to be further from the truth instead of nearer. The more we say about anyone the less we really know and understand that person. That is why I prefer to create a personal mythology about Suknaski and Shevchenko and put them into my life in a way that seems right for me. Living in that self-created translation that gives both poets a special meaning for me is more comfortable than viewing them in history or biography. The truth I assign to them becomes a part of my identity as a writer and that is the identity that I am most concerned with.

I remain convinced of the importance of Andy Suknaski to Western Canadian poetry. The image of him that I created is framed on my study wall like a religious icon. For me Andy is the patron saint of my writing, overseeing all my words—the truthful ones and the lies. Early on in my writing life I decided to write primarily about Western Canada, to be a devout Western regionalist, and Shevchenko had no role in that world. But then Andy came along. He represented what I believed in and fought for— the rights of the ordinary person, of workers and farmers. He was the Western Canadian identity in all its populism and radicalness. As I write these words at my computer his image stares down on

ANDY SUKNASKI

Woodcut by George Melnyk.

me over my right shoulder the way the icons of my Ukrainian Catholic childhood did when I was in church praying. In church, icons created a universe of their own for me to inhabit. Their stern, oval faces, their names in Greek letters, some printed on brightly coloured vestments, created an aura of complete symbolism, an ancient sacredness. My study where I write is now my new sanctuary and I have adorned it the way I remember church— with icons, symbolic masks and pictures, like the woodcut of Andy. That is what every writer must do—create a sacredness out of their own symbols, build a myth that becomes their faith and their meaning. It was perfectly normal then that my experience of sitting in Zion United Church in Moose Jaw in the summer of 1998, listening to Rudy Wiebe and Yvonne Johnson being interviewed by my friend Dennis Gruending while the spirit of Big Bear hung above us, involved Andy Suknaski sitting next to me. Here we were, two middle-aged parishioners, saint and sinner, offering our prayers in the holy church of writing, listening intently to the disembodied voice of a woman speaking from prison in the far southwest corner of Saskatchewan, speaking about pain and love with all the power of a Mary Magdalene. With Andy there are always miracles.

Another aspect of Suknaski's meaning for me is the Western Canadian tradition of alienation, of being marginalized politically, economically and culturally within Confederation. Within the region there is a great sense of victimhood, of disempowerment. Suknaski expressed alienation and disempowerment in his poetry and in his life. It is a model in which poverty, racism, violence, death and destruction are real. As well as ethnic alienation there is madness. Madness is a part of my myth of Andy Suknaski. A figure from the Slavic imagination that deals with madness is the figure of the holy fool—the one in the village who is outside the mainstream, who carries wisdom and understanding in spite of his nonconformity and his inability to be normal. To imagine the poet as a holy fool seems sensible, especially in the act of poetry.

Another version of ethnic madness was expressed in the 1960s, when there was a brief thaw in the Soviet repression in Ukraine, and a feature film was made whose title is translated into English as "Shadows of Long Forgotten Ancestors." The film described a village wedding in the Carpathian mountain region of Ukraine near my father's home. The film is full of religious icons but ends in a blood-splattering axe murder. In my final year as an undergraduate at the University of Manitoba I enrolled in a Russian intellectual history course whose textbook was titled *The Icon and the Axe,* symbolizing the polarity in Slavic culture between life and death. To me this course was an intellectual exercise until I met Andy Suknaski and he told me of how his mother had surrounded herself with a host of icons, not painted ones but saintly pictures taken from religious calendars because she was poor. He also said that his peasant father had once tried to take an axe to his mother. His father had come to homestead in southern Saskatchewan just after the turn of the century. The icon and the axe migrated with Andy's people from Europe to Canada. The peasant axing in the Ukrainian film and Andy's own family story are part of the same reality. Our cultural roots and images travel through space and time, the way those three books have travelled for me, and they come to rest in my consciousness, either on the surface or buried very deep. Ultimately, they determine our identity as writers.

Just as I cannot let go of the three books, which symbolize the three countries of my identity, I cannot let go of literary heroes and saints. Both are aspects of my literary identity. When

I chose to be a Western Canadian writer writing about the Western Canadian identity, as I have done for twenty-five years, I thought I was leaving behind my Ukrainian background. I thought I had the power of choice. I told myself that I didn't want to live in a Ukrainian universe, and yet I didn't want to live as someone totally assimilated to the official Anglo mythologies of the country I had come to live in either. So I chose to pursue the elusive goal of a new regional identity. I believed that the only country in which I would stop being a foreigner (since I was a foreigner in all three national identities—Ukrainian, German and Canadian) was a country of my own imagining. It would be a new country whose people had chosen to express a new collective identity. The West would be that country if it could break out of its subordinate relationship to Canada and express itself in a complete and autonomous way. I failed in my pursuit of that goal. I was unable to remake the real world after my own image and to satisfy my own needs. History, thankfully, was not on my side.

The failure to achieve a new society in the West has driven me back into myself and the images and identity I inherited without choice. Because of that historic failure I have found a new richness, a seemingly infinite source of wonder generated by the self and an understanding that is full of personal meaning. Now, instead of working to change history and society, I work toward greater self-understanding, hoping the exploration of the self that I have been engaged in will be of benefit to others.

In recent years I have become intensely autobiographical, linking my inner life with the external world that has been given to me and over which I have no control. I cannot shape the world. Instead I feel how it shapes me. This has liberated me from my original mission to change the course of regional history. So I feel free to accept the home I have been given and the self that I have inherited. My internal world seems so much more interesting for me now than the external world.

At one point in my writerly life I saw the progress of my adult life in terms of four symbols. The first was that of the wolf-buffalo, which was a description of myself I first used in a poem I published in 1972. A few years later I used it as the logo for NeWest Press. It still appears on the title pages of NeWest Press books. The second symbol was the turtle, which I adopted from aboriginal mythology as the creature that held up the four corners of the world, Turtle Island, the aboriginal name for North America. The turtle is a slow-moving creature. Today I am still a turtle holding up my world and considering it from below. Should I ever stop being a turtle I imagine that I would be a dragon. As a dragon I would draw on Chinese mythology concerning dragons but also the Christian imagery associated with my name. The Chinese dragon is a symbol of longevity, while in Christian mythology the dragon is a sign of fire and brimstone, of excessive and dangerous energy that must be kept from being destructive. The final symbol is St. George. I even commissioned an icon of St. George slaying a dragon, which also hangs in my study with a braid of sweetgrass over it to remind me of my destiny and the links between the aboriginal turtle and the Christian saint. St. George, who slays the dragon, is an obvious reference to the end, to posterity, to death because the self is destroyed by the self. Is this a reference to suicide? To sainthood? Or simply to the phase after life? What is most curious to me is that, without my intending it, the symbols progress from a mythic creature (the wolf-buffalo) to an earthly creature (the turtle) to a creature of the earth and air (the dragon) to a heavenly image (St. George).

TURTLE MASK

*George Melnyk covering his face with his turtle mask (paper maché
created by Tom Proudlock and painted by Sheena McGoogan.)
Photo: Julia Melnyk.*

This four-part symbology is a personal myth that combines European, aboriginal and Asian elements. It is utterly idiosyncratic. I suspect many writers have such idiosyncratic mythologies. Whether that mythology is true or prophetic is not important. What is important is how mythologizing creates identity. It is the way we talk to ourselves and understand ourselves. When my father took me and my brother to look for old books on Roman and Greek mythology in the Goodwill store in Winnipeg many years ago, he could not have imagined how important mythology would become for his sons. No matter how bizarre our personal mythologies may appear to those on the outside, they make perfect sense to us because they are composed of elements that we have invested with meaning. A personal myth provides a metaphor that pulls together all the elements of our lives. It encircles us and creates a kind of home. That is why writers need to take the sacred objects of their lives and the literary saints of their existence and create a mythology for themselves. The events of history that we have lived through and the myths perpetuated by family stories combine to become the muscle and bone of our self-expression. Never underestimate the power of hidden identity, of all those conflicting half-truths that we have created, all those memories and interpretations that forge our own story. In the end they are all we have and we will never live long enough to savour them completely.

The elements that we put into a personal myth come to us in mementoes like those three dog-eared books from my youth or in dreams or in pictures that evoke a world that we once inhabited. This miscellany of unpretentious objects and images carries deep secrets only for ourselves. They can sit for years, seemingly lost to our minds, and suddenly confront us with their power. I never know when those three Ukrainian books will face me again, challenge me with their history and force me to look inside myself and ask, Who are you?

———————————

Why I Am Not a Good Ukrainian:

A Family Fable

ASSIMILATION IS A NEGATIVE WORD BECAUSE it is about power. It deals with force, the weaker taken over by the stronger. It is about dominance and subordination. It is about place and culture and the cultural occupation that marginalizes other cultures. It is about the people of a place living the dominant reality, of being pulled by demands like nails clustered on a magnet.

Born of refugee parents in another country of a culture that was alien to both that country and to the one my family eventually adopted, I have been living assimilation all my life. It is ongoing. Although the metaphor of the nails and the magnet is apropos, my story is a curious one because the nail magnetized by the dominant culture seeks to transform itself into something else, a screw perhaps. It wants to turn. It wants to change—not in the way the dominant culture wants it to adapt but in a way that resists, that seeks to affirm the foreign, the immigrant's origins, since it is the "native" of the foreigner that is called into question.

Transformation is a more subjective way of dealing with the objective reality of assimilation. It seeks to return a degree of self-determination to the individual. Transformation, like assimilation, is about identity and about the creation of a new identity. While assimilation is about the power of place, transformation is about space, the room an individual needs to create new forms for the given content of life—family, language, culture and class—and to synthesize a shape that is both social and individual. In transformation the individual is both determined and self-determining. The determined element is the given of that person's life, all that they did not choose, while the self-determining is the meaning and understanding that person gives to the masks of their existence. The tension between assimilation and transformation is permanent.

Assimilation is often considered negatively by ethnic communities that seek to affirm their traditions and heritage. They see it as an affront to their inherited dignity and self-worth because assimilation means the triumph of dominance and the rejection of what had been given earlier. What defines ethnicity is precisely what is surrendered in assimilation—customs, language, different values, even religion. And yet every ethnic community adapts to the foreign culture around it and each community seeks success for its children in the dominant society. Assimilation is always a matter of degree, and retention of subordinate cultures is also a matter of degree. It is pure compromise. Those who adapt well survive and those who do not die out.

Curiously, assimilation does not result in the elimination of difference because there is no such thing as total and complete assimilation. Memory and family stories do not die. They may be submerged for generations but eventually the old identities resurface. Differences persist. Not only do they persist, they also transform the dominant culture. As ethnicity is absorbed it actually modifies the mainstream universe, transforming it into another reality.

Carl Jung stated that without history there is no psychology, that every person lives in the context of history and carries a history within them, a history not only of the wider world and events of that world, but a history of the personal experiences that have moulded them. In every moment of our lives we are surrounded by history and history is always being made; the present is continually turning into the past. A letter written becomes a letter sent and a letter sent becomes our history.

Every individual possesses a formative history that is part of their personality, their psyche. When an individual looks at their own history and tries to understand that history, they develop a story, a myth that explains to them what happened in life and how those happenings moulded them. By doing this they are transforming themselves, giving themselves a shape, a structure, creating a vessel in which they place their own contents and define themselves. Of course, there are those who prefer not to be self-reflective and take their definitions from others. They want the world around them to tell them who they are. But even those who reject self-determination always have an alternative thought about themselves, one that is out of harmony with the views articulated by outsiders, if for no other reason than the inherent inability of the outside world to know all our secrets or to fathom our true feelings. There is always an internal defining unknown to others.

I was born a displaced person in Germany after World War II. The term "displaced" is peculiar because it suggests an out-of-place experience similar to an out-of-body experience. One is placeless, but of course one is never placeless when one is alive. So begins the contradiction. One is placeless and not place-less. The placelessness refers to being in the wrong place or an inappropriate place or a place where one is always a stranger. *Displace-ness* is a form of homelessness and suggests a loss of identity. From the start the displaced person is a person whose identity is granted by others. The power of definition remains outside one's control. It is always someone else defining you.

The other term used at the time was "refugee." The refugee flees from one place, one country to another, forsakes one identity for the safety of another place or another country. Flight or motion is another attack on place. One is displaced by being a refugee because one has forsaken place for reasons of personal safety. One has chosen to flee place in order to live in another place. The relationship between refugee and place or a displaced person and country is the defining one. When the displaced seeks a refuge, he establishes an internal and an external duality in his identity. There is no oneness to be had. One is always disunited; one never has a singular wholeness to grasp. The country that one leaves is abandoned and that hurts. The new country is embraced, not for its inherent and comforting identity, but for its value as a refuge. Its identity is problematic as is its language, its people and its history. And if the displaced person lives in more than one new country and experiences several displacements, the problem is compounded. This is the problem of finding a place for oneself in a society that is not one's place. The primary cultural identity is provided by the family one is born into and even when that identity is modified by historical circumstances, the birth-identity remains embedded in the self.

For the adult immigrant the problems of settlement and adjustment never end, but for an immigrant child whose personal experience does not extend to the place where the parents were raised and yet who inherits their culture, language and religion, there is a duality different from that of the parents. They were formed by a single culture in another place, while the child's life is formed by dual cultures from the start—the inherited culture of the homeland the parents came from and passed on, and the dominant culture in which the child was schooled and moulded. The parents' struggle began in adulthood, when they were already formed, while the child's struggle was problematic at birth.

Displacement and refugeehood rest at the origins of my existence but not at my parents' origins. They are both Ukrainians who became refugees and immigrants later in life. I was born into both identities. If it is origins that determine us until death then my origin as a refugee and a displaced person is unshakeable. That beginning will haunt me till the end. No matter how Canadian I become in the eyes of others, in my own eyes I will always be a displaced person. Their origin is placement, while mine is displacement. As I meet new people throughout life they express a certain amazement that I wasn't born in this country. They usually say they don't detect an accent, which is what they associate with immigrants. The displacement I carry within is invisible to them.

Raised in a Ukrainian-speaking household in Winnipeg, a city where English was the language of education and society, I started out aware of being different, of being only partially assimilated. I was also raised in the mythology of domination and subordination, of imperialism and colonialism. My Ukrainian-born parents had already lived in a country ruled by others. Ukraine was part of the Austro-Hungarian Empire when my mother was born. Then it was part of Poland, which ruled western Ukraine between the wars. Then came Russian imperialism followed by German imperialism, and, after my parents fled, it was under

Russian control once more. My parents were born and raised in a political universe in which they were always part of a majority population ruled by others, and their region had minority status in the larger national or imperial entity that controlled it. That storied history was the history they imparted to me. Its issues eventually became my issues but in a different way, in a non-Ukrainian-centred way.

Because Winnipeg was a city with a large ethnic Ukrainian population going back to the turn of the century, my family life was as Ukrainian as it could be. We attended Ukrainian churches, Ukrainian cultural and political events and clubs. Our general practitioner and dentist were both Ukrainian-speaking. My parents took out the mortgage on their home through the Ukrainian credit union, and, of course, our family meals were determined by the ethnic cooking my parents knew best. Most of our social life was tied to an energetic ethnic universe.

Thirty-five years after first arriving in Winnipeg I moved to Calgary, having lived in other cities in the meantime. Calgary is a place with a small Ukrainian population. Here I live in an English-language universe, teach Canadian Studies at the university, write books in English, am married to a non-Ukrainian and have a son to whom I never speak in Ukrainian or have ever passed on any Ukrainian folklore, customs or traditions, in spite of my wife's encouragement. Whenever I visit my parents in Winnipeg, usually on my own, I speak Ukrainian with them and glance through Ukrainian newspapers they have in the house. I become what I was forty years ago. My parents have not tried to make their grandson conscious of his Ukrainian side. To them he is a Canadian for whom their Ukrainian past need not matter. How did this happen? Why is this the end result of the process of displacement, assimilation and transformation? Why am I not a good Ukrainian?

When I was a young man I felt I had three distinct possibilities. The first was retrenchment into my Ukrainian identity. The second was flight from ethnicity. The third was a new identity determined by neither given identity—the Ukrainian or the Canadian. I chose the route that offered more potentiality than reality. The way to escape the either/or was to say neither/nor. Of course, that meant creating an identity from a variety of sources, blending elements into a whole meaningful to the self. Considering the eclectic political universe my parents inhabited until they were in their early thirties, I could have confirmed that eclecticism in my self or I could have reached for a new singularity.

I embraced the idea of Western regionalism as the solution to my problem because it was not a displacement since I had experienced the West as place since I was three years old, and because its singular identity contained both duality and multiplicity. Western regionalism contained the duality of the region within the nation, while its multiplicity was the multicultural universe of both the historic post-contact world and the settlement period. For the immigrant refugee seeking a new identity it had everything. For two decades I pursued that identity, writing about it, creating cultural vehicles for its articulation and realization, defending its ideological validity in a hostile climate. I realize that this mission was rooted in my origins as a refugee child and my embracing the only place (the West) I have known as a home. The Ukrainian identity that my parents brought with them and passed on to me remained a placeless nationality, an idea rather than a country. Yet the Canadian identity that I received in Winnipeg was one that also made me unhappy. I couldn't identify with it either, especially since its parameters were formed by thinkers outside the region. Canada was Quebec

and Ontario and their history, which wasn't mine. I had to identify with a place and that place was the place I knew best, the West.

By choosing a Western regional identity I was able to express
both my Ukrainianness and my Canadianness. I replaced the
hyphenated Ukrainian-Canadian with the similar but unhyphen-
ated Western Canadian. My parents came from western Ukraine,
a region with a colonial history distinct from that of the rest of
Ukraine. This region was under non-Russian control for a long
time, while eastern Ukraine was a Russian colony for several
hundred years. I was predisposed to understanding regional differences. It was the way the family viewed the world.

Likewise, our membership in the minority Ukrainian
Catholic church made us distinct from the Orthodox Christianity
of the majority of Ukrainians. I grew up on my father's stories
about Polish oppression and imperialism by Russia and Germany.
So I was sensitive to issues of colonialism and imperialism from
the start and could quickly identify with, once I had learned of it,
the historical struggle of Western Canada for equality within
Confederation. It made Ukrainian sense to me. Being raised on
Cossack folktales predisposed me to Metis buffalo hunters.

The Canadian aspect of regionalism was even more obvious. Once I realized that I came from a hinterland region,
the story of that region in Canada and the history of Canadian
political evolution became crucial. I wanted to be a true Western
Canadian and to do that I had to identify with its distinguishing
features—the tradition of protest and rebellion. I found myself in
Alberta in the early seventies, at a time when the province was
beginning a decade-long battle to assert its right to economic
control over the price of its natural resources, a battle it eventually
lost. My regionalism was an accident of my personal history
because I certainly would not have been a regionalist if our family

had moved to Toronto, but it was also a free choice, one I made to fit the circumstances because there were many others in the region who didn't care about regional identity. Regional ideology was the space that allowed me to identify with a place. But I was just carrying on in a different context my father's Ukrainian nationalism, for which he was jailed by the Polish authorities just as the Polish state was crumbling under the Nazi Blitzkreig and Soviet duplicity.

But why did I choose this option out of the three I had? I could just as easily have gone another route. The other options have been chosen by others and they have worked well for them. My younger brother chose a different option though we had both been raised in the same milieu. He remained true to his Ukrainian heritage in his work as a composer, while I, as a writer, went off to fill my void with regional identity, something that meant nothing to him. He has spent a significant time in Europe, first marrying a Swede and then a Ukrainian. I have continued to live in Western Canada for most of my adult life. His music has celebrated and mourned the tragedy of Ukrainian history and its struggle for independence, while my writing deals with the cause of Western Canadian regionalism. Sometimes I think our choices are based on our names. His name is Lubomyr and he has kept that name throughout his life. It means lover of peace. My name is Yuri, but when my parents came to Canada it was changed to George, as the translation of my Ukrainian name. If I had remained Yuri, as my brother has remained Lubomyr, then I might have felt the power of foreignness much more and been closer to my Ukrainian past. The name George was a kind of Anglo mask I could wear while my brother had no such opportunity. Since his name was hard to pronounce in English, he was called "Lube" for short, not exactly a suitable English-language name. That he ends up in Europe, where the name Lubomyr works, and I end up in

BROTHERS

George (left) with his younger brother, Lubomyr, having a bath in their house on Pacific Avenue in Winnipeg, 1952.

Western Canada, where George works is not surprising. But what is important is the continuing displacement. Neither of us lives in the newly independent Ukraine.

But the differences between us are rooted in the similarity of our lives as children and young men and that similarity often breaks through the seeming differences. We were both raised on the myths of Ukrainian history, its heroes, its icons and the tragic course of its struggle for self-determination. Even when Lubomyr took to expressing all that in his music, he did so as a certain kind of outsider, the son of an émigré, a refugee, a displaced person. His children by his first marriage live in Sweden and are both Canadian and Swedish. He himself lives in both countries. After Ukraine became independent in 1991 he maintained cultural relations with it but never moved there. Somehow he preferred a continuing duality, just as I have. He is a Canadian composer and a Ukrainian composer living from time to time an exiled existence in Sweden. In spite of my efforts to unify myself under the rubric of Western regionalism I have been unsuccessful because that regionalism has continued to be a dualistic (Western and Canadian) identity.

In the case of my brother this dualism has been European and Canadian, while mine has been within Canada. My dualism goes even deeper than the refugee/displaced personhood we share. Its first source is in the very roots of Ukrainian identity, which even today lives within a bifurcated framework, created on one side by two centuries of Russification in eastern Ukraine, and on the other by the imperialism imposed in western Ukraine by the Austrian, Polish and finally Russian powers. Its second source lies in the multicultural life of Western Canada with its various ethnicities.

I have transferred this sense of dualism into a theory of Western regionalism that introduces the concept of the Metis metaphor as the essential expression of that regionalism. All Western Canadians live the Metis metaphor because its basic claim is that the region is informed by duality—aboriginal cultural existence in a technological universe, Anglo life in a post-modernist reality, and Canadian national identity struggling for relevance in an era of continentalism and globalization. The people of the region struggle to create a unity out of their own diversity. That is the meaning of the Metis metaphor.[27]

Multiplicity as the root of an identity has allowed me to combine a variety of symbols to express this metaphoric self. On the walls of our home hangs art by Western Canadian artists, some of Ukrainian background such as the visual poet Jars Balan of Edmonton or the artist Don Proch of Winnipeg. In my study there are symbols rich with dual meanings, such as pussy-willows, the adopted pagan sign of spring used by Ukrainian Christianity as a symbol of rebirth at Easter, and stalks of wheat, the grain of both Ukraine and Western Canada. Both the pussy willows and stalks of wheat stand in a wooden vase with carved folkloric designs my mother brought back from Ukraine in the 1990s. On the wall is a small icon of St. George. Curled around it is a braid of sweetgrass. Diagonally across from it is a cross made of faded bits of wood and wire from a deserted homestead in northern Alberta. To it I've attached a medallion picturing Madonna and Child. All three objects are dualistic, combining two elements into a unified statement.

This is the synthesis that has been the project of my life, the project of adapting the given to the created and making something new and different from what is old and established. In the political realm this project has not worked, but in the intellectual and cultural realm it has been successful. The self-understanding that duality provides me offers security and peace.

Out of that sense of peacefulness comes an answer to the displacement of the beginning. Trying to originate something new, to begin a tradition rather than simply inherit one and pass it on unchanged, is an act of transformation. Self-transformation has been my weapon against the power of assimilation. I have tried to remake myself through my own vision. The sense of place I have sought has ended up existing more in the realm of ideas than in a concrete reality. It has been a projection of my dream and has remained at that level—a projected dream. I had sought place but in fact I find that as a displaced person the most I can find is space to imagine, to create, to dream, to build a universe that does not exist. Displacement is the reality that drives my quest and denies its realization. Displacement has given me a dreamed universe to inhabit.

The Five City-States of the West:
A Prairie Fantasy

*"Let us create a city from the beginning...
Its real creator will be our needs."*

Plato, *Republic II*

IN OUR CULTURE THE GREEK CITY-STATE OF THE eighth to fourth century B.C. is the classic model of democratic urban life. Cities such as Athens, Sparta, Thebes and Corinth created sovereign political entities whose centre was a city. In fact the root of the word "politics" is the Greek word *polis*, which meant "city-state." The competition between these city-states was intense. Their most famous non-violent competition was the Olympic Games, while their more violent relations were expressed in various wars amongst themselves.

Culture was a key aspect of city-state life and the competition among city-states. The great names in classic literature— philosophers like Plato and Aristotle, playwrights like Euripides and Aristophanes, historians like Thucydides and Herodotus— were part of a great cultural outpouring that included architecture and the visual arts, sculpture in particular, in which the natural human form was celebrated. Added to this was a vast system of mythic gods and creatures handed down from the time of the legendary Homer. Their names have entered our European cultural consciousness and stayed there for millennia.

The intellectual and artistic achievements of the Roman Empire, which carried on the culture of Greece, were impressive, yet it was not until the time of the Italian city-states a thousand years later that a spirit of innovation, enquiry and artistic revolution known as the Renaissance matched that of the Greeks. Again it was the city-state that provided the context in which the arts flourished. The smallness of the city-state seemed to encourage innovation and the diversity of city-states brought forth unorthodoxy, while imperial systems like Rome's oriented their thought to system-building and centralizing through the creation of a superficial ideology of control.

The names of cities such as Venice, Florence, Milan and Rome are associated with such great names in Western art as Botticelli, Michelangelo, da Vinci and Titian; writers such as Petrarch and Machiavelli; and great patrons of the arts such as the Medicis and the Borghese. The Italian city-states were a creation of Mediterranean commerce and banking, shrewd politics and visionary cultural values. Wealth was the driving power that summoned a new era in Western civilization. It's worth remembering that the words "city" and "civilization" have their roots in such Latin words as *civilis* and *civitas,* which referred to urban citizenry and the importance of the city to identity, both cultural and religious.

Issues of wealth, political power and the need for local artistic expression are also present in the histories of prairie cities. Although they are not city-states in the classic sense, their geographic proximity, their historic ties, similar social roots and traditions express a unified reality also present in the Greek and Italian city-states. They share a common geography and language that allow them to identify with one another as well as express differences.

Thinking of Winnipeg, Regina, Saskatoon, Calgary and Edmonton as counterparts of these historic city-states may seem far-fetched—and it is if we try to equate them with the Greek or Italian city-states in terms of cultural achievement—but the exercise is helpful if we try to think of these five prairie cities as playing a role in the West similar to the ancient city-states in terms of being a ground for artistic expression in the region. It is in the prairie cities that prairie culture is most often exhibited, staged, televised and taught. These five urban centres were and remain the key players in regional culture, even though in the earlier agrarian-dominated period they were more conduits of cultural values than originators. Their competitiveness and their rising and falling status vis-à-vis one another is simply a confirmation of a history similar to the Greek and Italian city-states, when Athens rose to pre-eminence, as did Venice much later on.

The idea of viewing the five cities of the West as "city-states" comes out of my own experience of the region and its cities over the past forty years. I have been a Westerner and an urban dweller all my life, having lived for extensive periods of time in Winnipeg (eighteen years), Edmonton (thirteen years) and Calgary (fourteen years), while being a frequent visitor to Regina and Saskatoon. During this time I have been disappointed to find the limited role that the cities of the West play in the dominant mythology of the region. Compared to the Metis buffalo hunter or the sunburnt farmer on his tractor, images of the Western city are almost an afterthought that expresses some kind of inauthencity in relation to the region.

The contradiction between the region's urban heritage dating from the agrarian period and stereotypic agrarian images is worth exploring. A book of photographs about the region, *Prairie Dreams* by Courtney Milne, is a perfect example of the forgotten status of the city. There is not one urban image in the book. The message is clear: the prairie identity is rural. Period. Prairie refers to only the land outside the city. The prairie and the city are poles apart. Rethinking the region in terms of a group of city-states would redress the balance, undermine these traditional stereotypes and help Westerners recognize the future of the region as the urban-centred phenomenon that demographics tell us it already is. Why must the prairie city be at odds with prairie identity? Why must it be considered out of place when it is in place, when it stands on the prairie and shares in its identity?

The attempt to exclude urban life from the image of the West is rooted in a deep, anti-urban bias that runs through our heritage and has its roots as far back as Roman times, when the city was portrayed as a source of intrigue, decadence and indulgence, while the countryside was heralded as the home of virtue. Christian religious fundamentalism enhanced this attitude by denouncing cities as the source of sin, where temptation and vice lurked for the unwary innocents from the countryside.

This bias imprinted itself on the prairie mind. Not only were prairie cities full of dangers, but they were also derivative, nothing more than re-creations of nineteenth-century Eastern Canadian cities. There was nothing original here, just a carbon copy of what was already established elsewhere. The soul of the West was in the countryside. Western Canada's leading urban historian, Alan Artibise, claims the opposite—that prairie cities have a character all their own.[28] They are cities with broad streets, a predominance of single-family homes and low-density housing, a sense of spaciousness that reflects both the flat prairie landscape and the newness of cities begun from scratch no more than a century ago. They are cities for whom transportation corridors are their main raison d'être and where immigrant and speculator, entrepreneur and worker, banker and farmer have fought for survival and success. They may be new cities based on late-nineteenth and early-twentieth-century economic needs, but clones of Toronto they are not. The Canadian historian J. M. S. Careless has focused on the historic origins of Western cities as "creations of the railway."[29] This isn't completely accurate because Winnipeg and Edmonton pre-date the railway, but it is true that the railway turned them into cities. He calls them "urban outposts" of central Canada, even if their urban character is different.[30] He views them as a string of cities along the forty-ninth parallel expressing the East-West character of the Canada created since Confederation.

Since prairie cities developed with the mass migration promoted by Canadian authorities in the late nineteenth century, there is a tension between their indigenous character and the central Canadian vision of them as a corridor of Anglo-Canadian culture and society. The provincialization of the region into Alberta and Saskatchewan in 1905 limited urban power and influence by making municipal government a subordinate, a third tier of politics below the federal and provincial governments. A city-state structure for the West would reverse this political hierarchy by placing the city at the top. With the city-state, nationalism and provincialism would disappear. A European observer of contemporary national identities argues that "the past was always cities as well as 'countries'...the descendants of the city-state may be the city-states and city-nations of tomorrow, redefining political autonomy, and nationalism..."[31] Will the twenty-first century be the age of new city-states?

In the bitter cold of December 1949 my father's arms carried me down from the coal-fired, smoke-belching transcontinental train that had brought my family to Winnipeg from the port of Halifax, thousands of miles to the east. Our transatlantic passage had been on a converted troop ship that was filled with survivors, refugee immigrants seeking a new and safe life.

We were part of a brief upsurge in postwar immigration to the West that was really only a trickle compared to the great human flood of a half-century earlier that had inundated the region with eager, homesteading pioneers. Careless makes the iconoclastic observation that prairie urbanization had proceeded then at a faster rate than rural settlement of the West.[32] The figures are worth noting—38 per cent of Alberta's residents were urban dwellers in 1911 (the height of the early agrarian period) and the figure for Manitoba was even greater—43 per cent.[33]

When I began my life as an urban Westerner I was part of a significant population in the region who were not farmers. All my childhood and youthful memories are urban and all my adult experience is likewise urban. I see the West through urban eyes— the eyes that see brick and concrete towers, imposing mansions and clapboard row housing, diesel buses and freeways, and ubiquitous suburban lawns.

This is the way millions of Westerners see the region. Out of a population of about 5 million in the three prairie provinces, almost 3 million live in the five major cities. If we add the populations of smaller cities like Lethbridge, Red Deer, Brandon, and larger towns like Fort McMurray and Thompson, over 70 per cent of prairie people live in urban settings, and that percentage keeps growing annually. How could a social and economic reality that includes two out of three people be excluded from the region's imagination? This is only possible because city life has not been associated with the region's identity in any major way.

In the period of agrarian settlement city-dwellers were an integral part of the region's formation, and now they form a dominant part of that identity. Careless has pointed out that "...the urban West was decidedly a fact of life before 1914..."[34]

Even though our lineage goes back to the beginnings of white agrarian settlement, we city-dwellers continue to think of ourselves as strangers to the prairie identity. To paraphrase Gertrude Stein, a city is a city is a city. Is regional identity purely land-based? Is geography the only element to offer distinctness to a people? It would seem so. But what about the pre-urban, pre-railway, pre-agrarian period of the aboriginal peoples, the Metis hunters and the fur traders?

In 1858 H. L. Hime, a Toronto photographer with the Assiniboine and Saskatchewan Exploring Expedition, produced a series of photographs of the West that capture that pre-agrarian moment on the verge of disappearing. What is striking about each image, whether it be St. Boniface Cathedral or walled Fort Garry, is the sense of isolation that the stand-alone buildings have. Prairie space dominates. The buildings speak more of intention and aspiration than reality, more of absence than presence.[35] For the white imagination, the West in the pre-agrarian period was simply emptiness seeking fulfillment. Hime's work is the visual equivalent of William Francis Butler's masterpiece of a decade later, evocatively titled *The Great Lone Land*. If one were to compare Hime's photographs to the colour landscape photos of Courtney Milne, more than a century later, one would sense immediately the rich variety witnessed by the contemporary eye as compared to the bleakness viewed by mid-nineteenth-century travellers who felt themselves to be on the edge of civilization. In the nineteenth-century West, the European eye was not only black and white in a technical sense but in a spiritual sense as well. For the white world the West was an opposing blackness. But in the twentieth-century West, the European eye saw only colour in the West—a bright, fecund universe that glowed with richness. Postcard beauty replaced the steel engraving.

The "urban" reality of the fur trade era, if we can even speak of such a thing, was the trading post or fort. It was the central meeting and trading place, where transportation, business and cultures intersected. The trading post prefigured the urban reality because it had connections to an international economy and it created a small, permanent concentration of population in a sea of aboriginal mobility. Of course trading posts were not cities, or towns, and often they were barely fit to be considered villages, yet their general character set them in opposition to the surrounding culture and lifestyle. When Western cities developed as part of agrarian European colonization they made the fur trading posts part of their pedigree.

In 1949 I stepped into a city that was the pre-eminent urban reality in the West—the *primus inter pares* of the five major cities of the region. Winnipeg gave my childhood and youth a sense of urban importance. By the time I was ready to leave in the late 1960s, that pre-eminence was fading as Alberta's cities began to take on a leading role in the region. The railway economy that had made Winnipeg a centre of small manufacturing, commodity and goods transhipment was in decline. In 1920, 60 per cent of the region's manufacturing occurred in Winnipeg, but by 1967 Alberta's manufacturing sector surpassed Manitoba's.[36]

I had come from Europe to Winnipeg by ship and train but when I went to Europe in 1968 I flew. This was symbolic of the new technological and economic forces that would change the power relationships among prairie cities. Accustomed to living in an urban environment, I was not surprised to find myself in Edmonton at the beginning of the 1970s. The seventies belonged to Alberta because its oil and gas reserves made it wealthy and powerful. It was a province with the largest population and throughout the decade it served as a magnet for investment and the generation of wealth that transformed its two major cities into the most powerful cities in the region.

What I brought with me from Winnipeg to Edmonton and later Calgary was a certain sense of what urban life is—straight, tree-lined streets boxed in rectangular grids, the "block" and "neighbourhood" and "corner stores" as the limits of community, the life of "the street" and "the back lane" and the amenities of public transportation and urban entertainment. Everything from schools to pools was in close proximity, as were people. The sense of "the crowd" and the largeness of multi-storey buildings and time spent walking on concrete sidewalks and driving on concrete streets are all integral to the urban experience. So are parks and green spaces and playgrounds. It is all a rich mosaic of experiences that ultimately made sense to my urban eye.

The city seems self-contained and self-sufficient, a world complete unto itself. To this can be added the history of a city, its ethnic neighbourhoods and multicultural life, its class divisions, its socio-economic hierarchy, its elites and its underclass. One quickly learns its special places and its danger spots. Cities change with history. They evolve, transforming themselves with each new influx and migration. After just a few decades, places are no longer the same. The city has changed and keeps on changing. Privileged neighbourhoods decay, dangerous ones become gentrified.

It was in Edmonton that I first imagined the West as a system of city-states because my involvement in literary publishing took me from prairie city to prairie city, visiting bookstores and writers. The NeWest project, a magazine and book publishing venture that I launched in 1975, allowed me to make spring and fall trips across the prairie and keep up contacts with each city's writing and artistic community. Through these contacts I saw how different the culture of each city was and yet I also felt a deep identification in each city with it prairie sisters. There was rivalry but also respect. NeWest was an urban prairie project and it is not surprising that its various parts eventually resided in three prairie cities, a symbol of regional unity.

Personal odysseys for urban dwellers (immigrants from other countries and regions, rural refugees from an increasingly concentrated farm economy, and migrants from other cities) are both very private and yet universal. The struggle to survive in the prairie city and to improve conditions for the next generation is balanced with the memories of childhood friends, school adventures and adulthood. For all those who have been long-term residents of the city of their birth and whose families have been urban dwellers for generations, there are an equal number who are first-timers and for whom an urban heritage is a pioneering experience, an innovation in the family tree.

In the early days of the prairie city, the main themes were boosterism and urban rivalry as various centres vied with one another for prominence.[37] It was an age of city-building. In the case of Calgary, Saskatoon and Regina it was building from scratch—creating a city on top of the prairie soil where only grass existed. This founding and building process began about 1880 and was complete by 1920. "In the booster era, the era of the commercial and early industrial city," Alan Artibise writes, "there was an identification by the booster elites of their fortune with the fortunes of a specific community."[38] Each elite tried to attract capital and workers to its locale. Paul Voisey, writing about early urbanization, described Winnipeg as "a glittering example of successful town promotion."[39] At the turn of the century it far outdistanced other prairie cities, generating wealth and jobs. It was the gateway city, the bottleneck through which people and goods entered and departed the region.

Artibise tells us that this "booster" phase was replaced after World War I with a spirit of "corporatism" that lasted till after World War II. In the corporate phase the founding elites had secured their status, their enterprises were growing and the institutions of government and commerce were headquartered in the urban core. Although the Depression struck at many of these private fortunes, the cities continued to be a source of capital, enterprise and connections. The business of the region flowed in and out of the cities because the elite who managed it resided in the cities.

The most recent phase in urban life is termed "regional" by Artibise. He sees the cities as developing their own urban-centric economic and social identity through the provision of key services in health, education and finance for their own residents and the surrounding locale. We can imagine these cities as radiating concentric circles of power with some overlap. Lethbridge is in the sway of Calgary, while Red Deer is divided between Calgary and Edmonton. The dual-city phenomenon in Alberta and Saskatchewan creates an interplay between cities, encouraging transportation and communication between the two centres as business and government go about their affairs.

Think of prairie cities as magnets that both attract and repel, pulling and pushing constantly. Their strength is in their ability to influence smaller places and repel the influence of other cities, and so create a distinct identity. No one confuses Saskatoon with Regina or Calgary with Edmonton in terms of their social, economic and cultural identities. They are entities in their own right with a spirit all their own. It is the critical mass of a city's political economy that gives it a character, that makes one city distinct from another. This divergence is rooted in the differing origins of each city in the agrarian period.

Voisey describes the symbiotic relationship that existed between rural settlement and the spectacular growth of prairie cities when between the turn of the century and World War I the population of the West quadrupled and the needs of this population had to be met by cities and towns. "The growth of the cities... was an economic response to massive rural settlement," he writes.[40] It was not surprising in Voisey's view that Winnipeg should grow so fast, since southern Manitoba had been the most densely settled part of the region.

In 1881 the Canadian census registered Winnipeg as the only "city" in the northwest. Its population was 8,000. Thirty years later its population was 144,000, Calgary had 44,000, and Saskatoon 12,000.[41] Sixty years later Winnipeg had 540,000 residents, Calgary 400,000, and there were 126,000 in Saskatoon. By the 1980s Winnipeg's population was being surpassed by Calgary and Edmonton because of Alberta's economic expansion in the 1970s, which attracted people from all over Canada to these two booming centres. By the mid-1990s the combined population of Edmonton and Calgary had surpassed 1.5 million.

The social composition of prairie cities in the early period encompassed a broad and diverse spectrum: 25 per cent of working people were in the professional or service occupations; 20 per cent in trade and merchandising; 20 per cent in construction; 15 per cent with the railways; an equal percentage were in manufacturing, and 5 per cent in finance.[42] As prairie society developed, each city evolved specialized features. Winnipeg's role as a railway hub diminished as airplanes replaced trains for passenger transportation, and its role as a financial centre dropped behind Calgary as agricultural marketing became less important. Calgary's role in the capitalization of oil and gas increased in the sixties and seventies but then faced downsizing in the eighties, while Regina and Edmonton developed bureaucracies linked to their being the seats of provincial governments. In the nineties Calgary boomed once more.

These differing economies and roles resulted in a lack of pre-eminence for any one prairie city during the past thirty years. Obviously the young of Saskatoon and Regina (and in my case Winnipeg) did move to Edmonton and Calgary in the boom times, but the basic balance and symmetry of the five city-state system has remained. No great new city has arisen and no one city has collapsed. Winnipeg may have fallen behind Calgary and Edmonton, but Winnipeg remains a gateway to Western consciousness, with some of the richest cultural life in the region. A realignment of power has occurred but that is a natural historical progression. It is an evolution, not a revolution.

Two factors are important in maintaining this "steady-state" reality. First, the physical distances between the cities are sufficient to allow independent development of a hinterland linked to each one. The distances are also large enough to encourage the development of indigenous institutions such as galleries, museums, sports arenas, etc. Second, the cities themselves are "small." There is no great metropolis on the prairies that overshadows other cities. Edmonton and Calgary balance each other as do Regina and Saskatoon, while Winnipeg is circumscribed by the political economy of Manitoba. Small cities tend to develop a full range of cultural, social and economic services, which may not always be of the highest calibre but which allow a broad spectrum of local activity. They are cities with populations big enough to justify having their own universities, for example, but small enough not to dominate neighbouring cities. Cities tend to feast on themselves, herald their own activities, self-centre.

Not having a New York or Los Angeles means that there is a decentralized feeling to the region that suits a confederational model of city-states. For a century the five cities have provided the basic framework of urban distribution in the three prairie provinces and that model has not changed dramatically during that time. What would be required to upset this system would be some fundamental economic or political upheaval that would re-orient the basic nature of the region. Such a change is not likely in the immediate future.

Because the West does not have a "world-class" city or dominating metropolis, its urban centres enjoy a certain equality and autonomy that cities existing under the shadow of metropol-itan centres in other countries do not. With areas of older housing that attract an ever-changing mosaic of immigrants and refugees, the cities of the West are constantly being reinvigorated by new populations.

Visible minorities are a growing force in Western cities as Canada reflects new patterns of immigration both foreign and internal. Immigrants traditionally settle in cities where they can find government services, educational facilities, employment and fellow immigrants. Aboriginal people, especially in Regina and Winnipeg, are an expanding population seeking new opportuni-ties for economic and social growth. All of this continues to give prairie cities an internationalism and multiculturalism that they have had from their beginnings.

The city-state is not a common reality in the world (Singapore is the most famous now that Hong Kong is part of China). Yet its future may be more welcoming than its recent history. Currently the nation-state remains the benchmark for political status. A country with a capital city and a land base is the norm. But that does not mean that other forms of sovereignty will not arise in the future. The current tensions in established states may require novel solutions. The unification of Europe and continentalism in

North America have undermined national boundaries and national authority. The tension over Quebec independence has produced various formulas for restructuring the country should Quebec leave. These pressures influence political thought in Western Canada and raise questions about the possibility of a post-provincial system of government in the region. Would not a confederation of city-states be a viable option?

Historically, the provincial system of government was a creation of geography and history. A country as large as Canada, it was argued, could not be centrally governed solely through the instruments of a national government. The "federal" concept recognized the division of powers between provinces and Ottawa and so the provinces became a basic unit of Canadian identity. In turn provincial governments balanced rural and urban interests, trying to represent both constituencies and their needs. In the provincial system, small rural populations are able to exert power vis-à-vis the more populous urban areas. In a city-state system, the primacy of cities would be recognized and rural interests would be subordinated.

Would there be advantages to the rural areas in such a system? I believe there would be. The map of the region would be redrawn. Alberta, Saskatchewan and Manitoba would cease to exist. In their place would be a region divided into five city-states, having all the powers that the three provinces now have—five provincial capitals if you like. The rural inhabitants in each city-state would relate to the capital city and the smaller centres under its control linking their economic future to that of the city-state. It makes more sense for a beet farmer in southern Alberta to have Calgary as his seat of government than Edmonton. This move would allow a mixing of private and public roles for each city rather than one place being the "government town."

Unfortunately this vision will not work because it does not mesh well with the geography of the region, whose northern, non-agrarian areas are far from most urban centres created on the plains due to agrarian settlement patterns from a century ago. What would one do—allow Regina's territory to extend almost up to Saskatoon's boundary because Saskatoon would be responsible for everything to the north? And what about Winnipeg, which so dominates Manitoba? Such a political model would leave Manitoba belonging to Winnipeg.

No, this little fantasy will not work, but the purpose of the exercise is valid—how to imagine the city in the West in a new way. Alan Artibise tells us, "Canadians are an urban people. More than 75 per cent of the country's population lives in cities."[43] Westerners are an urban people like other Canadians. This fact must be recognized. At some point the city has to become a dominant power in both the cultural and political mythologies of the region because the reality of the cityscape has to spill over into our self-understanding and self-actualization. The current political structures are a product of an agrarian age of rural dominance. That approach is no longer valid, but the Western city has yet to take its place of prominence in our mindscapes.

In the search for what is truly Western, the prairie city has been systematically ignored and set aside. This has been an exercise in self-denial because the urban reality has been with the West from the time of European agrarian settlement. It is time for that self-denial to end. The land cannot be the sole arbiter of our identity, just as the farmer can no longer be the core of its mythology. We have been obsessed with the land and its meaning for us for over a century. Perhaps it is time to reflect on the cities we have built and seek to understand how our identity is expressed through them.

If the city-state cannot be the core of new political boundaries, then can it be the core of a new self-understanding and a way of seeing the region in which the local designation of Calgarian, for example, is more important than the designation of Albertan? Certainly it can because what binds the city-states is regional history and regional geography and what separates them is that very same history and geography. That they have been made subordinate to the provincial identity and provincial politics with their rural bias does not mean that they need to continue to do so in the future.

Regional identity has given the cities of the West an inferiority complex. They have been caught in the vise of an urban-denying identity rooted in a glorification of agrarian settlement a century ago. The city is the technological hub of cyberspace, the new geography of the twenty-first century, and it is this geography that is transforming who and what we are. A regionalism centred on the concept of the city-state is more in harmony with this new digital geography.

The Urban Prairie:

Between Jerusalem and Babylon

MY WESTERN CANADIAN IDENTITY HAS COME to me through city life. I'm used to concrete towers, brick buildings, asphalt streets with long rows of houses, traffic jams and crowded malls. I'm not the only one. This is the way the majority of Westerners see the region every single day and yet that experience is viewed as incompatible with the agrarian myth of the region. The experience of city life from childhood to adulthood has moulded millions of Western Canadians but it is considered inauthentic compared to the genuineness of rural existence. The continuing self-image of the region is one of endless prairie fields or grasslands with their icons of farmers and cowboys holding us in its sway. The reason for this is obvious. The wheat farmer and cattle rancher are icons because they reflect the distinguishing feature of the region— its prairie geography and a livelihood tied to it—while the Western Canadian urban reality is viewed as the same as that of other cities. If you want a regional identity you have to take it from the land and not from the city. The land is distinguishing while the city is not.

An important example of this thinking is Sharon Butala's best-selling non-fiction book, *The Perfection of the Morning: An Apprenticeship in Nature* (1994). The book glorifies life on the land:

> *I found solace in the extraordinary beauty of the land itself. On a warm spring day riding a horse, walking or travelling in a truck across short prairie that had never known a plow in all its history since the glaciers, I thought I had never smelled anything so wonderful in my life...*[44]

For Butala and her many Canadian readers, most of whom live in cities, humanity can only find itself in Nature, and the city has overpowered Nature. This division between light and darkness means that true humanity and the Western Canadian identity are rooted in the land and nothing but the land. Literary critic and writer Ian Adam of Calgary describes Butala's worldview as being made up of contrasting determinants.[45] She works in polarities. Cities are an ugly and evil scar, places of poverty, suffering, marital break-up. In contrast, the land is full of beauty and perfection and mystic power. This is not only Sharon Butala's vision but the vision shared by many Western city dwellers. We see our home as something unpleasant, as inappropriate and lacking in perfection. The city is a kind of pox on the landscape, devouring nature with its artifice. This is a kind of urban self-loathing. If you fantasize about the beauty and genuineness of nature, you must condemn urban life as unnatural, polluted and artificial. This thinking has been with us ever since the Romantic vision promulgated at the start of the Industrial Revolution, with its "dark, satanic mills." But anti-urban bias has been around a lot longer than a few centuries. Western Canadians are simply continuing a grand tradition going back to the Romans. Adam points out that frequently it is "university-educated authors who create these rural icons of place."[46] While Butala describes her post-rural conversion visits to cities like Calgary as stifling, Adam points out that many rural dwellers come to the city for relief from country life just as city dwellers seek emotional and spiritual renewal in the country. Although each community seeks its opposite, it is the rural that holds sway over our imagination.

Our culture has set landscape above the city. The city and the land are opposites in which the city is negative and the land is positive. That's the myth we live by. Historical fact is a little different. When I began researching my earlier essay, "The Five City-States of the West," I discovered that urban life went hand in hand with the development and growth of agrarian society at the end of the last century. We created cities in the region at the same time that we settled it agriculturally. They were not an afterthought, a late development. They happened at the same time. They were co-inhabiters of the landscape. And as for nature, didn't the farmer change the ecology of the natural region through agriculture in an even more dramatic way than did the establishment of cities? Butala writes about ranching in southwest Saskatchewan, an enterprise in which cattle approximate the role of earlier ungulates like bison on wide-open grasslands, at least, until the last stage of a penned-in feedlot, where free-range cattle end their lives. The cow-calf operation may be romantic with its vast vistas and endless sunrises, but the next stage of feedlots and abattoirs is not.

If we can acknowledge the negative aspects of rural life, why do we deny cities a positive place in our cultural imagination? Admittedly, cities lack something "open" and "free" and "natural" that exists in an agricultural landscape. There is boundless prairie space uncluttered with concrete and glass towers and rows of suburban housing. That is where Butala captures the dreams and feelings of the human spirit. Her book takes us out of enclosed coffee shops and boutiques, out of office buildings and factory assembly lines, out of artificial electric light and carpeting and puts us in rolling hills, grass, endless sky, our bodies in touch with the body of the land. How can we not be drawn to her vision?

Urban dwellers are constantly in motion toward non-urban nature be it a lake in summer, a ski trail in winter or a mountain path. We are drawn to an opposite reality that rewards us with its "naturalness." But is the countryside all that opposite? And doesn't the Western Canadian city contain more nature than we imagine? Again a factual representation of urban ecology in the West may not meld with the myth of the West we hold so dearly. When one thinks of the perpetual cycle of chemical farming that is the essence of the grain industry, of the air-conditioned megatractors that allow two men to farm ten square miles of land, of the farm animal factories where milk cows, hogs, and chickens are scientifically raised, one can see urban values on the land.

So much of the art and the literature of the region has been dominated by rural images that it has entrenched the dichotomous relationship of city and nature in our consciousness. It is as if the cities of the West did not matter to our identity or they were somehow anti-Western simply by being cities. The argument about the sameness of all cities is false because cities are distinct from one another. Paris is not London and London is not Mexico City, though all three have subways. As social and historical constructs, cities are unique entities with their own genetic codes. Our prairie cities may have come into existence in the same time span but they feel different from one another, attract different people and carry on different activities. In fact, Western cities form a kind of inter-urban balance that has evolved since their foundation. Their relationship has defined the region. But Butala is not arguing sameness in *Perfection of the Morning*, she is arguing the deep distinction between city and countryside, between nature and the unnatural or human-made. For her the division is profound and it is a division in which all cities share no matter where they are located.

Besides the attitude of "all cities are the same" and equally harmful to our souls, there is another basis for the negativity toward cities. The biblical tradition is ambivalent about urban life, viewing it both as the sacred city of the temple, the holy city, which may be called Jerusalem, and also as the city of corruption and evil, which may be termed Babylon. The city is both Jerusalem and Babylon. This Manichean division into black and white is rooted in the earliest myth of the Bible—the garden of Eden, which is paradise. Paradise is nature itself, pure and unsullied, while the city is the opposite of paradise. The city is full of intrigue and the artificial because it is a product of humans. Nature did not create the city, we did. It is full of hubris where humanity structures a social and architectural order in its own failed image. By being driven out of the garden of Eden, humanity has set itself against nature. We produce sinful places like cities, while nature is pure and innocent. What we have built and created stands in opposition to the natural order. Christ is tempted by Satan with an image of cities of gold. The Bible denounces cities like Sodom and Gomorrah while it raises Jerusalem to sacred status. This thinking was reflected in the desert fathers, early Christian monks who glorified escape from the temptations of urban life to rural solitude. But this negativity about the city contrasted with another early tradition, that of the Greeks, which praised urban life as the essence of the human spirit.

In the pre-Christian classical tradition, the Greek city-states were held up as great models of human life blessed by various gods as the centres of the human community. The *polis* was the epitome of society. In the time of the Roman Empire the city became ambivalent once more, with Rome seen as decadent and oppressive, while the countryside held honour and virtue.

The theme of urban corruption continued into modern times when cities like London and Paris were viewed by their national cultures as dangerous places where all manner of sin existed and which people of good character avoided. One could not be pure of soul in the city. It is this view of the city that we have inherited and that colours our culture to this day. The land is romanticized and the city is presented as a plague.

The anti-urban bias that we have inherited through the ages is deeply rooted in the popular psyche. In Roman times it was the freehold farmer who was considered the repository of Roman virtue. In the days of England's royal glory, the sturdy yeoman was praised as the salt of the earth and the source of national strength. Sharon Butala, in our own day and in our own region, decries rural depopulation and dreams a great vision of the right way to live. She says:

> If we abandon farms and farmers as we have known them for the last ten thousand years, we abandon our best hope for redefining ourselves as children of Nature and for reclaiming our lost souls...[47]

After living on the land, she can no longer stand the city. So what of us, who live here, who may actually enjoy life here? Are we somehow less than the people described by Sharon Butala? Are we somehow morally impoverished because we live in cities? After reading her book one can be excused for feeling that cosmopolitanism is the essence of alienation. Yet with the farm population of the prairie provinces below 10 per cent and heading toward the national average of 3 per cent can we say that 90 per cent of the people who live here live the wrong way?

The Urban Prairie

It is time to balance this negative view of city life with a more positive one in which nature and the city are not incompatible opposites and in which urban people are shown to be as much in love with the land as rural people. The urban ecology of Western Canadian cities is not just concrete; it is often an amazing source of natural life that replenishes the spirit.

A century ago, when farmers were transforming the landscape from native grasses and parklands to wheat and barley, we had five major urban centres—Winnipeg, Regina, Saskatoon, Calgary and Edmonton. A century later we continue to have those five major cities. They have been here for a long time and they have not destroyed the landscape, only transformed it in their immediate locale. In every case these cities have created large urban forests where there were none and created a natural ecology filled with wildlife—squirrels and raccoons, magpies and swallows; even beavers have returned to the cities of the West. During that time the energy source for these cities has evolved from wood to coal to fuel oil to natural gas, becoming less environmentally hostile with every technological transformation. From the beginning nature has been part of the urban landscape in the form of parks, river valleys, grassy schoolyards, playgrounds and sports fields.

In the fast-growing city of Calgary, where I live, nature is everywhere. Within the city boundaries, there are an estimated one to two thousand deer and over a thousand coyotes. In my own inner-city neighbourhood, which is a fifteen-minute walk from the downtown skyscrapers, there are nesting peregrine falcons, and when I walk the five kilometres from my home to the university, the whole distance is either in green space or along shaded residential streets. Vast natural areas such as Nose Hill Park in the north and Fish Creek Provincial Park in the south create a wilderness feel within the city. And the Bow River, whose riverbank is protected, cuts a huge swath of nature through the city. In my rides along the bike trail that extends along the Bow I always encounter Canada geese, myriads of ducks of various kinds and numerous other birds, including orioles, waxwings, warblers, sparrows, wrens, meadowlarks, swallows and thrushes. My favourites are the cormorants. One time I even saw a bald eagle gliding over the river valley next to my home. Occasionally bears and cougars get caught in suburbia and moose become urban trespassers. In recent years the University of Calgary campus with its manicured lawns has become home to a resident population of deer. For a time the ridge near our home had a family of grouse that travelled back and forth along the bluff that marks the former banks of the Bow.

As an urban dweller I spend a part of each day in the "nature" of the river valley and it has taught me the importance of nature to my life. Butala and I share a love of nature. What I don't share is her belief that the city is antithetical to nature. Perhaps if we returned to the ancient view of the Greeks praising urban life we would be able to overcome the dichotomy that our culture teaches. If we thought of the city more as Jerusalem than Babylon we would enter a new way of appreciating our urban surroundings.

Mircea Eliade, in *The Myth of the Eternal Return,* wrote how cities and cosmology are linked:

> *...all the Indian royal cities, even the modern ones, are built after the mythical model of the celestial city...man constructs according to an archetype...[and] this participation by urban cultures in an archetypal model is what gives them their reality and their validity...*[48]

Where is Calgary's mythical archetype? The glorification of the ranching life in the Calgary Stampede is the city's association with the landscape, not Calgary itself. Edmonton's archetype is Klondike Days and the heroic trek of gold miners to the Yukon.

This identification with the rural past approximates Eliade's process of archetype at work. Further in the book Eliade explains how a city is made sacred through its mythology:

> ...*because of its situation at the center of the cosmos, the temple or the sacred city is always the meeting point of the three cosmic regions: heaven, earth and hell...So Babylon (in its own tradition) is the city built where heaven and earth meet and (in the bible) the rock of Jerusalem is described as reaching deep into the subterranean waters (which reflected chaos before creation).*[49]

For the ancients the city was the centre and as the centre it was the zone of the sacred. But Western Canadian cities like Calgary are viewed by their residents as secular, commercial places with no sense of their having any sacred place in the universe. Certainly nothing as sacred as Sharon Butala's claims for a mystique of nature, which exists only outside the city.

But there are places in the heart of our urban life that are good for the soul. Contrary to Butala's worldview, nature penetrates the city and provides a natural centre for the human spirit. It is through river valleys that Western Canadian cities like Calgary, Edmonton, Winnipeg and Saskatoon create a sacred centre. In Regina's case it is a creek and an artificial lake. In Western Canadian cities nature penetrates to the core of the city and city people come to the natural centre to regain their spirit. Many do it on a daily basis. Many Calgarians are not divided from the natural or its sense of the sacred the way the stereotype of the city would have us believe.

The Romans spoke of the *mundus*, the world, as a trench that was dug around the place where a city was founded and where the divine, the terrestrial and the subterranean met, creating the centre of the universe. Calgary is a centre for those who live there. Their days revolve around it. It is their sanctuary and their temple, and their lives and occupations are reflected in its image. The image of a trench is more intriguing than the image of a walled city of our heritage.

City dwellers also go out onto the land, sometimes a hundred thousand strong on a single summer weekend in Calgary. We go out to Sharon Butala's world because it is not the city and city dwellers feel a need for otherness. But that otherness, which we covet because it lacks buildings and innumerable people, is often a re-creation of urban technology, whether it be a ski resort in the mountains or a relative's farm with its television and Internet. The transformation of the countryside is relentless and the preservation of natural wilderness areas is a constant struggle for environmentalists. In a sense everything is now contained by human effort, everything natural is somehow now a park, except for the wilderness in the northern half of the prairie provinces that has so few people.

Rural people come to the city for their urban needs as urban dwellers go out to the country for their rural needs, even if it is to just pass through countryside on the way to another urban centre. That doesn't mean that city and country are pure opposites and that one is good and the other bad. It means that there is a difference but one that we should not colour with inherited morality. We are dealing in degrees not absolutes.

There was a time in the history of the West when some prairie people talked about the region as the home of a New Jerusalem, a heaven on Earth, a visionary utopian place where the good life could be lived and the perfect society built. It was an ideal that has never come to pass. But its makers did dream a sacred place. Is it possible to make Calgary or Saskatoon a sacred centre when its current mythology is closer to Babylon than to Athens? According to Sharon Butala it can't be done. The only true paradise is Nature writ large.

Calgary has nature writ small within it, a sacred centre, a meeting place of different worlds, a coming together of all forces that make up life. For the urban dweller a city like Calgary can become sacred in the act of planting and tending a garden; it becomes sacred when one is on Nose Hill, looks at the mountains and feels the chinook wind; it is sacred when we offer up prayers in the city; it is sacred when we stop and listen to the birds sing or watch the ducks and geese from Prince's Island.

The anti-urban bias of our culture has created a false polarity. It sees the human on the land as a minor intrusion and the city as a nasty way of making the human dominant. It seeks to bring us back to a world in which the ecology of the garden of Eden is permanent and unchanging, and human activity is not transforming. Yet the city represents change and adaptation by deer and skunks, porcupines and coyotes, which continue to inhabit natural urban spaces. In places like Banff, which has an urban-like development, elk prefer lawns to wild grasses. Although the natural is secondary to the human-made in the city, it is not absent. That secondary presence in material or physical terms does not mean that it is less important. It is the presence of "the other" within us. It is a constant reminder of our biological origins and needs. The waters of the rivers that exist at the centre of these cities nourish the inhabitants and actually make those cities possible.

As the home of most Westerners, the city is the dominant social and economic reality of the region. By honouring the city we honour ourselves. We make a place for ourselves in the prairie

landscape in the same way that cities make a place for themselves
in that landscape, upright figures in a great open space. We are
wrong to think of cities in a one-dimensional way, as nothing but
highrise, concrete jungles. This is a distorted image inherited
from our anti-urban culture. If we continue to view the urban
prairie solely as an interloper on the beauty of the natural landscape, as the opposite of rightful living, as the enemy of true
humanity, then we will be a people alienated from ourselves, from
our very centre, and we will be unable to live without guilt and
self-hatred, which are the ultimate conclusion of the anti-urban
myth. If we treat cities as an original sin, then we will always feel
doomed to search after what is outside the city to save us. Only
people who are comfortable in themselves and true believers in
their identity can have a positive self-image. Butala's work is just
one of the examples of how much of our contemporary literature
is profoundly anti-urban and self-destructive. We have forgotten
the central reality of the city as the archetype of the universe and
a blessed place.

If the city can become for each of us a sacred place, if it can
be a place where mythic time is regenerated and history overcome, if it can somehow become the celestial city of the Vedic
scriptures, or the place where eternal struggles of good and evil
are fought and where myth lives, then the condemnation of
urban life that we have come to believe will be put aside.
Of course, it is only each one of us, in little ways, in small acts of
personal ritual and simple, prayerful thoughts, who makes the
urban prairie a sacred place.

One corollary of the anti-urban myth has been the belief
that true community exists only in rural communities—small,
discrete, intimate kinds of places, while the city is the antithesis of
community. Of course, that corollary is as false as its main premise.

Cities are composed of communities, a great variety of communities and neighbourhoods, whose residents feel at home in their "part" of the city. These communities have their "high street" where commerce is carried on. They have their own schools, playgrounds, parks and places of worship. Here the community meets, interacts and celebrates. Of course, not all interaction is tied to one community, just as a small town in a rural area may have several churches from various denominations. Urban dwellers identify with their small communities in the city. These neighbourhoods are their villages.

The demythologizers of the urban prairie like myself seek to strip it of its exclusively negative connotations and dress it in robes befitting a place that is a centre of a universe. To imagine each Western Canadian city as being built around a holy spring around which the urban universe turns, rather than as a place of unnatural darkness, is a way to cultural freedom. Why shouldn't we rethink ourselves in this way? The urban prairie is still the prairie, and as long as the natural prairie remains an integral part of urban life in the West, the city can call itself a sacred centre of regional identity.

Coming to Matador:
Dreams of the Soil

NESTLED IN THE GENTLY ROLLING COUNTRY of southwest Saskatchewan is a special place—a small circle of houses and outlying farm buildings that belong to the Matador Farm Pool. The word "Pool" has been used for decades to describe the great agrarian co-operative movement that was launched in the 1920s in the three prairie provinces, when individual farmers "pooled" their grain production into co-operative marketing organizations.

The precursor of the Matador Farm Pool was the Matador Co-operative Farm, one of a series of co-operative communities established in the late 1940s and early 1950s under the guidance of North America's first "socialist" government, the Co-operative Commonwealth Federation (CCF) led by Tommy Douglas. Co-operative farms were an experiment in co-operative living and co-operative production that went far beyond the philosophy of the marketing pools that had been established in the 1920s. While the Pools gave farmers economic power, co-op farms gave them a co-operative economic life.

Matador has a patriarch. He is a compact, athletically built man who enjoys organic gardening and a solar-heated greenhouse-cum-hot tub that he has added onto his 1950s stucco bungalow. His name is Lorne Dietrick and he has been at Matador since its beginning in 1946. I first met him in the mid-1980s, when I was writing *The Search for Community*, a book about the global co-operative tradition that included a proposal for a new kind of co-operative community for Western Canada called a "social co-op."

Because Saskatchewan's farm co-ops were the only indigenous form of co-operative community that the region had experienced, I was keen on meeting these pioneers. Lorne Dietrick was already retired when I met him. He was a founder of a dream, guardian of the Matador story and interpreter of the co-operative farming tradition that arose at the end of World War II. He was the one who divided the world into friends and enemies of co-operation.

The first effort at co-operative farming in Saskatchewan began at a place called Round Hill in 1943. The Round Hill Agricultural Co-operative Association was a machinery co-operative in which a group of farmers invested money to purchase machinery to be used jointly on a rotation basis. In March 1945 the Sturgis Farm Co-operative Association was incorporated with nine members and 3,000 acres. It was the first example of a full co-op farm rather than being simply a machinery-sharing co-op. The members of Sturgis were established farmers who pooled their land, livestock and equipment. They worked together and they shared in the fruits of their collective effort.

The older, less radical tradition in farming that led to the establishment of wheat pools confirmed the private ownership of farms and individual production. It restricted co-operative activity to bulk purchasing for the benefit of members and marketing of members' grain through their own organization. In opposition the co-op farm idea rejected private property in favour of co-operative property and it also rejected the single-family lifestyle, preferring intentional community life. Co-op farms were a socialist initiative.

They had the blessing of the new CCF government, which was anxious to offer aid to returning war veterans in harmony with its own ideology. The government called a series of meetings at which it offered assistance to those who were willing to farm co-operatively. It came in the form of free Crown land, loans for operations and technical assistance. Here was a fresh government, unencumbered by history or precedent, that wanted to do something different. The Department of Agriculture, the Department of Reconstruction and Rehabilitation and the Department of Co-operation and Co-operative Development were all involved in making the scheme work.

In his memoirs, Dietrick, the first president of the Matador Farm Co-op, describes rather drily how he got involved in the movement:

> *In the winter of 1945 the Government made available the first tract of provincially-owned land for veteran's co-op farms. This was the old Matador ranch in south-western Saskatchewan. The future members of the Matador co-operative farm came together at a conference held in Regina April 6–9, 1946...Fifty veterans attended. We were told that each veteran was entitled to 480 acres in southern Saskatchewan and 320 acres in the north...*[50]

He had served in the Navy during the War and was then a young man of thirty. The other founding members who took up the CCF offer were also demobilized veterans, mostly young, single men.

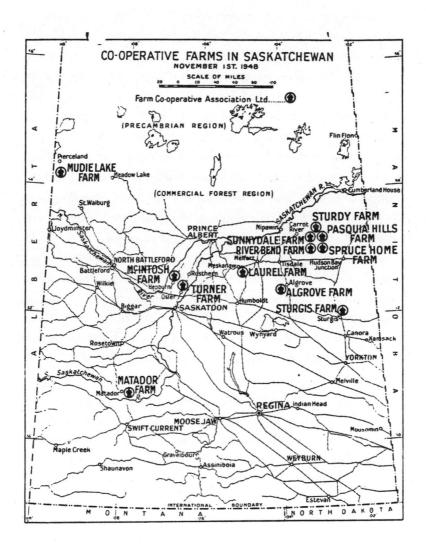

CO-OP FARM MAP

Co-op farm map published in 1949 by the Government of Saskatchewan.

This group of veterans immediately began the process of creating a community at the former cattle ranch on the South Saskatchewan River. They were going to be pioneers, not only as sodbusters, but also as practitioners of a dream, a vision of a left-wing, co-operative–centred life. A 1949 pamphlet issued by the Government contains photos of these early days—a line of men planting a row of saplings on the bald prairie; a requisitioned quonset hut being pulled on-site by a tractor; the first farm homes standing in a semicircle like denizens of a incomplete suburb. Matador received 10,000 acres of prairie grass, but the *Veteran's Land Act* did not allow the federal government's grant of $2,320 per veteran to be pooled co-operatively. It was meant only for private property. So the provincial government made up for the lack of federal grants with its own money repayable at 3 per cent interest. The veterans had a thirty-three-year lease on the property with an option to purchase after ten years. The rent was one-seventh the value of the crop. With about $40,000 in capital and the goodwill and support of the provincial government, the seventeen men of Matador began their pioneering work. Lorne describes how things got going:

> *Our membership was made up of single and married people. We decided that the married couples should have a home and a lot for their own use. The single men would live in a dormitory...The first year we were able to build the houses for the married couples and the dorm...*[51]

In 1948 the federal government relented and provided the veterans with their grants. The provincial government was repaid, but the federal government insisted that each co-op farm be limited to ten members in order to get the grant. Matador was split in two.

By 1950, 20 co-op farms with a total of 210 members were set up. The number of farms peaked at 32 in 1952. The average membership was 11 members. Added to this number were spouses and children, which resulted in a total of 30 to 50 persons living on a co-op farm. By the early fifties Matador had 63 souls. It was considered one of the premier co-op farms and was presented as a model community. Yet out of a total farm population of about 400,000 the co-op farm population stood at less than 1,000, a mere one-quarter of one percent. From this peak it declined. By 1972 there were only 11 farms reporting and their membership stood at only 61 members. The co-op farm idea, so revolutionary and exciting right after the war, became a slight blur on the social and economic landscape.

When I first visited Matador, four decades after it was founded, the original, rather modest bungalows had been replaced by large, contemporary ranch-style homes, expressive of contemporary social values and the economic success of the re-named Matador Farm Pool. Lorne and his wife, Kay, continued to live in their original home. Although expanded, it represented the values of the pioneering generation and its collective ideals rather than the achievement, material success and comfort of the succeeding generation. Of the few old buildings still standing was the one-room schoolhouse where Kay had taught. Its windows were broken; its former white paint was now grey and peeling, and nailed to its side was a worn, faded sign, "Matador Co-op Farm." The fact that this unused building remained standing like a lone sentinel of another era, while looking so forlorn, suggested the ambivalent attitude of the current Pool members to their fathers' generation. They both wanted and did not want to identify with those earlier beliefs.

A photo of the 1979 grand reunion of Matador residents and former residents and their children shows a large gathering that looks on the surface like a huge extended family. I wondered,

WELCOME TO MATADOR

The old sign at Matador. Photo: George Melnyk.

when I looked at that photo, what Matador would be like today if all these people were still here, and instead of a hamlet, there was a real village and a multi-generational community.

The women who had come to Matador as brides tried to recreate the single-family units to which they were accustomed. They were not interested in communal facilities and did not play a role in field work. Childrearing and housework were the main female activities at the time. These women wanted to fit in with the spirit of the wider society that pressed continually on Matador, and most succumbed to that spirit.

Economically, however, the co-op did well. The issue of land tenure and private ownership was always a little unclear because this was Crown land that was being leased. Each member had received a lease for 480 acres and then in turn that member leased his leasehold to the co-op. In 1956 the right-to-purchase clause in the leases kicked in and Matador faced its first major internal crisis. Three members decided to leave the co-op. They took the houses they had been living in at Matador to the neighbouring village of Kyle. The event was as painful as a divorce. In an article published several years after the split, one of the Matador women is quoted as saying, "We can't get used to losing Ruby and Beth...All of us feel as if a part of the life here was torn from Matador. It wasn't the women's fault. If it hadn't been for the women on the farm, we might have lost more in the crisis."[52]

While the co-op farms declined, the number of "production co-ops," which involved a limited form of machinery pooling or pasture sharing, increased from 52 in 1949 to 313 in 1964. Co-operation that did not involve community ownership and production and that preserved the sanctity of the single-family farm was the standard. Farmers wanted to increase individual profits through group activity but were not interested in socialized profits. The great experiment in co-operative living and ownership of land had not won the hearts of the people. And why should it have?

The experiment was a state initiative that veterans and a few ideologically motivated individuals joined. The CCF government gave the project credibility and guided it in the direction it wanted. The veterans' resettlement issue gave the matter both an urgency and social approval. But in a few years the veterans' issue was no longer pressing and the era of the Cold War was firmly entrenched in the North American psyche. Co-op farms were now too radical a concept. Earlier, during World War II, Soviet collectivization was a benign curiosity because the U.S.S.R. was an ally, but after the War it was painted as part of the grand horror of communism. Co-op farms became suspect.

Their quick rise gave them an initial impetus and momentum carried forward by a mixture of youthful enthusiasm and state subsidy. But the experiment never achieved a critical mass the way the Wheat Pools had with their hundreds of thousands of members across the prairies. Co-op farms never reached institutional status. They were always marginalized on the fringes of the farmer-created co-op movement of the 1920s.

Often viewed as ideological outcasts, co-op farms tried to fit into the political and social landscape of North American society. When Lorne took a public stance as a member of the peace movement of the 1950s, which many considered a front for the Communist Party, some members of his own co-op took out an ad in the local paper disassociating themselves from his views. When it came to politics there was no collective voice, only individual stances.

The slow disintegration of other co-op farms had a demoralizing effect on those who remained in the movement. Stress increased on the survivors as departure became more frequent and new members fewer. As the movement shrank, relocation to other co-op farms became less of an option. Matador became an island in a sea of single-family farms.

Acculturation and integration into the views and values of the wider society became the norm. The on-site school, which had played a role in maintaining co-op values, was closed in 1966 and the children bussed to outside schools. As well, these children were reaching the age of maturity and their future had to be considered. There was room only for those who wanted to farm. There was no other economic activity at Matador. Most left and were absorbed into the mainstream. Those who remained took over the Matador Co-op Farm through a new entity, the Matador Farm Pool, which allowed the founders to retire, get their equity out and their children to carry on. But there was no energy to found new farm co-ops or other co-operative enterprises. The NDP's Land Bank program bought the old co-op farm and the new Pool leased the land from the Bank. By the mid-1980s there were only 8 members left. Lorne and Kay continued to live at Matador, while one of their sons farmed. Their life was there. Every meaning, every hope, every disappointment of their adult life was experienced on the banks of the South Saskatchewan, a river that flowed like eternity through their all-too-human lives.

All the mechanisms of society are oriented toward conformity. Nonconformity survives only when it is strong, powerful and popular. Co-op farms had none of these attributes. They were more of a rebellion than a revolution. They failed to attract a constant flow of new adherents because they were viewed as an economic enterprise rather than a religious one. And the economic benefits they offered in later years didn't seem so special. The co-op farms experienced the general decline of the rural population and an increase in the average size of farm operations with less and less manpower. When Matador was formed, there were 130,000 farmers in Saskatchewan. By 1990 there were only 50,000. Only an ever-expanding number of co-op farms and an increase in the diversity of economic activities and enterprises could have made co-op farming a significant reality. Why didn't this happen? For example, why didn't Matador buy the neighbouring farm co-op at Beechy when it was dissolving? Instead a Hutterite colony purchased the land. Why weren't there new businesses established at Matador to employ people year-round and give a new vitality to the community?

There seemed to be no energy for such a strategy. The members didn't see this as part of their mission. After all, they were farmers and they followed the general evolution of farming. Even if someone like Lorne Dietrick believed the co-op needed to expand, there wasn't enough support among the other members, and the co-op was a democratic organization. The co-op seemed to be living only for itself, even as it shrank. The other co-op farms were no different. There was no charismatic leadership, no over-reaching ideological goal or vision. There was no dream shared by each and every member beyond that of survival.

In contrast, the Wheat Pools were a vital economic and political force because they enrolled so many farmers. They were institutionalized in a way co-op farms never were. Co-op farms were confused and divided and dependent on government support, not only initially but later on as well. They were children of a state initiative and they knew it. They didn't create the movement out of their own desires and hopes. They joined because of the economic opportunities it offered those who could not afford to start their own farms. It was a way to homestead just like their forefathers had. While religious groups like the Hutterites continued to expand their group farms, combining total self-help with religious sanction, the secular world and hazy ideology of co-op farms seemed to lead only to decline.

In 1944 the CCF was a radical government priding itself on its democratic socialism. Its successor, the New Democratic Party, inheriting the vicissitudes of the Cold War, preferred the comfort of social democratic thinking in which private property was fundamental and socialist property was an embarrassing concept. Throughout all this Lorne remained true to his vision. The isolation of Matador, hidden in the rolling hills of the distant prairie, is symbolic of Lorne himself. He stands alone, proud, defeated and unrepentant. A city person like myself feels nervous on the empty gravel country road that leads to this tiny bastion of collectivity. There are no farmhouses easily visible nearby. One comes up on this little cluster of homes and farm buildings unexpectedly. They surprise you.

The 1950s home the Dietricks live in is part of Lorne's commitment to the founding. It now looks out of place amidst the new homes of the Pool members. He and it remain a bridge to the early days, but few want to cross that bridge into history. He has positioned himself as the doorkeeper to the Matador ideal rather than its reality. He is the guardian of the dream. His idealism is as muscular as his own body and his devotion to Matador and socialism remains undeterred.

In the mid-1980s Lorne and I worked on his memoirs while I was a research associate at the Canadian Plains Research Centre at the University of Regina. Most of our relationship was on paper—handwritten manuscript pages from him and typed and edited pages from me. His letters were often in pencil on lined sheets, while mine were typed on letterhead. We belonged to two different worlds. I sat in my home in Calgary while he sat in his home at Matador. While I played the persona of the professional editor, he played the persona of the careful narrator moulding a story as he wanted it told.

Lorne was reticent to write about his pre-Matador life, as if it barely mattered, and in writing about Matador he was excessively impersonal, dealing with socio-economic issues rather than personalities. I kept trying to get him to open up about personal incidents of community life but to no avail. The story he wanted to tell was the story of co-op/state relations in which the state failed the co-op movement. As an actor in the story, he preferred to deal with impersonal forces rather than human interest. In this he was a true socialist.

Just before the completion of the final draft of the memoir I visited Lorne one more time. There had been no rain all spring. Everything was bone dry. At one point Lorne took me up to Matador's water source. The water for the homes was fed by gravity from a spring that was not on co-op property. Walking the parched land to the spring was my very first experience of the prairie beyond the yards and gardens of the hamlet. I was coming to the source of life at Matador and I was walking toward it with one of the founders of everything human that now stood here. The spring had figured in the choice of the original settlement site and Lorne was particularly pleased with the quality of the water. It made Matador a real oasis, not just a mythological one.

Lorne uncovered the dark well cover to check the water level. I imagined that he was peering into the past, into some kind of eternal mirror, where the reflection of Matador was always fresh and clear and where his own aging face was perpetually reflected. It was more than water to him; it was the very lifeblood of Matador. Its flow paralleled the flow of Matador's history. It was genuine, unpolluted and long-lasting, just like co-op farms were meant to be in his own mind.

That the spring was no longer on Matador land only reflected the cruel reality of historical evolution. The source of their life was not in their hands. It stood outside them and made them vulnerable. Lorne experienced that vulnerability for decades but it hasn't distracted him from Matador, his life's project. I suspect that Matador would not be a co-operative today if it was not for him. His intense belief in the experiment is expressed rather bloodlessly in these words from his memoirs: "the building of a co-operative society rather than a competitive one."[53] Such a simple phrase, but contained in it is the great division of the world as he sees it, between what he believes is good and what he believes is evil. As always he is committed to the partnership between co-op farms and the state. The last sentence in his memoirs concludes pessimistically that "if the privatization schemes of current governments continue there will be no co-op farms left by the year 2000."[54] He is everything that co-op farms were and were not.

Lorne approved of the role of the state in co-op farming. He felt that only a favourable government could sustain something as ideologically unpalatable as co-operative farming. Co-op farming was a child of the state, and when the state turned its back on the child, the child felt abandoned. Lorne is a political person. There exists a photo of him on a train in China in 1976, the year Mao died. It is a close-up of him looking out the window of the train. He is gazing intensely into the distance, his face in profile. It is a fitting photo for a visionary of group farming in a country where collective farming was the imposed norm for decades. The train and the well are the two symbols—the former of history on the move and the latter of eternal hope. On that Chinese train looking out the window is the true believer, the keeper of the flame of co-op farming moving through a historical landscape in which collectivity is the only reality. Here he could feel the unrealized dream from Saskatchewan quiver in the winds of a sister reality. While his true home is an isolated island of forgotten socialism, his imaginary home is here.

By the 1990s the great agrarian collectivizations of communism, the kolkhoz of the former Soviet Union and the commune of China, were receding as privatization became the new ideology of both Russia and China. The state upholder of collective values had changed its colour from red to blue. Revolutionary societies were melding into the privatized universe of global capitalism that Lorne had fought all his life from his little island of collective dreams in southwestern Saskatchewan. The great betrayal had happened. It was no longer just a tiny speck of social democratic history hidden in the far reaches of a distant prairie that was giving up on the dream, but the one-time vast power of communism itself. And yet, even when the war between history and the individual is lost and history has won out, the comforting strength offered by belief never disappears completely. To have lived a co-operative life like Lorne has is a privilege few have experienced in this country. The emotion of memory meets with the body of personal truth and together they beat at the heart of a life genuinely lived.

On Being a Self-styled Guru of Western Regionalism:

An Untrue Confession

A REVIEWER ONCE DESCRIBED ME AS THE SELF-styled guru of western regionalism. The phrase intrigued me because it carried so many resonances. To be called a guru was both flattering and derogatory. In our culture the word "guru" connotes expert knowledge and lofty position but it also signifies something alien and cultish. To be "self-styled" means a coronation in one's own mind, an identity one bequeaths to one self that others do not recognize. Without legitimacy in the real world, the self-styled guru is a figment of his own imagination.

The more I reflected on the phrase, the more validity it began to possess and the more truth it carried. Although I had initially felt slighted, I later came to understand that there was something here that cried out for exploration and meditation. Was I really self-styled? Was I a guru? What did western regional-ism mean now? What was it in my writings that gave rise to such an observation? What was it about my ideas that demanded this kind of comment? After two decades of writing on the West was the result nothing but a personal fantasy?

My mind turned inward, into what I had done and said. It began to analyze, to create the dim outlines of an intellectual autobiography. All because of this simple, and yet not so simple, description. Writers tend to be self-obsessed, to live inside their minds as they create sentences, characters, plots and eventually books. Our language flows from the concrete reality of whatever world we inhabit and from our innermost recesses, from the mystery of imagination connecting dreams, life and text. We style what we do; we have a style; we create a style; we struggle with form and content. To be self-styled is not such a terrible thing for a writer. But for a writer who struggles to create ideology, well, that is another matter. In the world of ideology and political ideas, the only thing that matters ultimately is realization, the word made flesh. The only ideology that deserves respect is ideology that is espoused and practised; it is ideology that has made history.

The radical regionalism that first formed in my mind in the 1970s was a corollary of the Canadian nationalism that was important to Canadian intellectuals in that decade. Radical regionalism espoused the anti-Americanism of Canadian left nationalism but it also espoused a pro-regional anti-centrism. It was both socialist and western. It was both anti-imperialist and anti-nationalist. It looked at the history of Confederation as flawed and it sought change. That decade was also the time of the great battle between Ottawa and the West over the pricing of natural resources, and the region was rife with resentment. So radical regionalism was also a corollary of that movement for provincial rights. But radical regionalism never went anywhere in terms of public support. It never manifested itself in a political or social movement. It was only an idea—one man's idea.

In the 1980s the ideology of radical regionalism, first expressed in a book of the same name, and its dream of an indigenous socialism came to rest in a rethinking of the co-operative movement in Western Canada. In *The Search for Community: From Utopia to a Co-operative Society* (1985) I suggested the creation of a co-operative community called social co-ops that would be a radical evolution of the co-operative tradition in the West. The book sold reasonably well and was even translated a few years later and published in Japan. But nothing happened. No social co-ops ever came into existence. As a child of radical regionalism the social co-operative was stillborn.

Nothing was realized other than a regional magazine and a publishing house (NeWest). But they were institutions that carried on their regional mandates without ideological direction from founding ideas. Now the guru, if he was one, had no ashram in which to preach his truth and to generate followers. For a few years I soldiered on with three books on the subject of the West (*Riel to Reform: A History of Protest in Western Canada, The Urban Prairie* and *Beyond Alienation: Political Essays on the West*) and a newsletter on co-operation that I sent to my friends. So my regionalist faith began to crumble and lose meaning in the face of historical change and decades of ideological irrelevance. I had turned fifty and began to sense that I was truly self-styled and nothing more.

It had all begun so grandly in my mind. First there was the cultural phase and its institutions furthering regional identity; then there would be the social phase of co-operative communities; and finally there would be the political phase when the ideology of indigenous socialism would spawn a political movement, with each phase building on the achievements of the previous phase, creating a seamless embodiment of radical regionalism. Nothing of the sort occurred. It turned out to be simply an idea. I had rung a bell of my own making but nobody answered. History went on its merry way.

"Only an idea" is a phrase that we often use to privilege reality over imagination, to value the material over the intellectual. For an intellectual, ideas are fundamental. They are both the tools of the trade and the arena in which to ply the craft. The ideas of an ideologist are only valued when they achieve a level of truth, that is, find themselves realized in the world in one way or another. Ideas need material confirmation to be valued. Otherwise they are fool's gold. When communism was the reigning ideology of hundreds of millions of human beings and the official religion of two vast states, the Soviet Union and China, it was reality and power. It had to be taken seriously. With the end of its embodiment the power of Marxism as ideology has slipped severely. Its credibility and its power to influence reality have been minimized.

Radical regionalism became a theory without a practice, and for ideology that is death. What happens to a guru whose theory lives only in unread books? What does a loss of faith mean to the founder of the faith? This has been the issue that I have grappled with since the mid-1990s and I've answered it in different ways. First, I've adopted the unflattering adage that those who can't do teach, so I have become a teacher, a lecturer in Canadian Studies. Second, I've poured my energy into a two-volume literary history of Alberta, a subject that is of the West but not encompassing of the region as a whole. In the literary history, I have adopted the voice of the postmodernism and postcolonialism that is the dominant literary ideology of my time. It is not the voice of radical regionalism. Third, I have had to deal with the psychological distress of no longer having a mission as I once did and of having to find a substitute to fill the void. I admit to the relativeness of ideology, of the great need to have one, any one.

The self-styled guru can either remain true to his original faith, to the ideological self he has styled, or he can surrender that identity, switch loyalties, give up on his own ideas and take on new ones that others have created. It hurts to change. And if the original ideological commitment felt like a perfect fit, like the right glove, then the substitute is never as good. It pales beside the memory of what was. The first true love isn't forgotten.

Who or what is responsible for the defeat? I can blame myself, say that I just wasn't guru material, that I didn't have what it took to convince others. One can also say that the ideas themselves were so bizarre or unpalatable that there was no hope for their adoption. They were simply out of place or time. Or I can blame history, the power of others, all the forces that exist outside myself. Like the European socialists of the early nineteenth century, who floundered in a sea of utopian ideals and schemes, the guru of radical regionalism became a casualty of history. The great neo-conservative revolution launched by Margaret Thatcher in the late 1970s, the end of communism and the Soviet Union in 1991 and the resulting dominance of American capitalism, and the birth of the information age are all macro forces that shaped the world and contemporary history away from any possibility of public interest in radical regionalism. In the end it doesn't matter what the reasons are for its lack of success. The situation remains.

And what about "western regionalism?" What has happened to it? How has it evolved since I first formed my ideas? The region has moved from the stage of post-agrarian protest that encompassed the provincial rights movement of the 1970s and early 1980s, the time of my original thinking, and has entered a stage of political economy that is continentalist, in which American trade and markets determine economic development more than any other force.[55] The old verities of agrarian protest politics, the romance of Third World liberation struggles, and the needs of the working class have been subsumed by the dogmas of fiscal restraint, anti-public spending and triumphant capitalism. The prime political vehicle of this continentalist regionalism is the Reform Party led by Albertan Preston Manning. In the 1970s Manning and I met from time to time and talked politics. He espoused a right-wing view of the West that encompassed the region from the Manitoba-Ontario border to the Pacific Ocean. As a former Social Creditor and the son of the Social Credit premier of Alberta, he was comfortable with a view of western regionalism that included British Columbia. I, on the other hand, represented the left and limited my regional identity to the three prairie provinces. In the mid-1980s he created the Reform Party and ran in the federal election of 1988, which was the election fought over the Free Trade Agreement with the United States. It was the first defining moment of the new continentalism.

Within ten years Manning had become the Leader of the Official Opposition in Ottawa and his party was a household name across the country. His strongest political base was in Alberta, where the party was headquartered, and in British Columbia. As a politician he had understood regional reality and he had used it successfully to make history. His view of the immediate future of western regionalism was correct and mine was wrong. He was successful because he held right-wing ideas at a time when the neo-conservative ideology was dominant and on the offensive. The ideas he held were those that were actually moulding society. My ideas had fallen by the wayside with a whole grab bag of leftist ideologies from social democracy to left-wing nationalism to communism. Only those political figures who could address the new ideological verities carried any credibility. Another Alberta figure, former publisher Mel Hurtig, tried to lead a new nationalist party forward in the early 1990s when the Free Trade Agreement was expanded to include Mexico, and he failed quickly. The audience for his 1970s ideas was minuscule. My own ideas on regionalism were left behind by a rapidly changing reality. Manning knew his political culture well; he was a doer, I a dreamer.

The political economy of the region had split after the post-agrarian phase and a new regionalism has emerged, with Saskatchewan and Manitoba continuing to retain an important agrarian identity, while Alberta moved closer to British Columbia in its economic profile. The American-fostered idea of Cascadia, which links the American states and Canadian provinces that share the Rocky Mountains (Alaska, British Columbia, Alberta, Idaho, Washington, Oregon and Montana) into a western super-region, seems to have greater relevance based on economic ties (and, in the case of British Columbia, economic battles, because Cascadia would be able to unite the interests of B.C., Alaska and Washington over salmon fishing in a way the two nations cannot). Calgary and Vancouver now have an hourly air shuttle like the one between Toronto and Montreal in the east. In the 1970s and 1980s the hourly airbus existed only between Calgary and Edmonton. It turns out that Manning was on the right side of history and I was on the wrong side. Right-wing populism included British Columbia, but radical regionalism did not.

While ideas are suspended in time, hanging like immovable clouds in the unchanging skyscape of a painting, historical reality is like weather, a state of permanent, never-ending flux. Only those ideas that fit the times have any currency and we only know which ideas they are after the fact, after they have proven their relevance. Since ideology is a way of transforming the world, the ideology that cannot transform is irrelevant, and the thinker of such an ideology has to accept the unpleasant fact that his thoughts don't count.

Where can such a thinker, having come to this realization,

find refuge or solace? The only place I have found that refuge is far from history and deep within the self. The articulation of a public dream is surrendered to the quest for personal mythology. The things that matter to the "writer-guru's" identity can no longer be the self-styled musings of irrelevancy; the things that now must matter are those that formed me from the beginning, the givens of every life—family roots, childhood memories, upbringing, the people and events that shaped and disfigured a life, moulding it into a vessel that is one's self-identity. The mask of the ideologist is dumped into the scrap bin of history. There remains only personal mythology and self-understanding. When history has turned its back on you what else is there but your personal self? Since the thesis of my literary identity has been a public ideology (regionalism), its anti-thesis is the thinking that is not for others but only for the self. My ideas become ideas that are true for me and are meaningful in the mythological universe that I inhabit. I write to convince myself and not to convince others. I speak out of myself and to myself, and any speaking that has meaning for others is a bonus and not an essential. This writing is the abandonment of history and the role of changing history after my own design. The publication in 1996 of my first book of poetry, *Ribstones,* signalled the new literary identity.

About the same time that this was happening in my life, a film version of the Booker Prize–winning novel *The English Patient,* by Canadian Michael Ondaatje, an immigrant from Sri Lanka, won the Academy Award for Best Picture. The film has come to represent my commitment against history, a value I have carried within me for thirty years. The film is a postmodernist statement—produced by American money, based on a Canadian novel, with a screenplay and direction by a Brit. The film is a new version of *Casablanca,* a World War II film that is considered one of the greatest of all times. In the U.S. *The English Patient* (the film) was denounced by some for painting a glowing picture of the real Hungarian count who spied for the Germans. In Canada it was publicly denounced by a philosopher from Calgary as being immoral. The morality of loving a woman and fulfilling a promise to her at the cost of other lives was not in the public interest. Unlike *Casablanca,* which was made during the war and extolled public need over personal desire, *The English Patient* damns both sides of the war and privileges the personal over the public. *The English Patient* made sense to me just as the film *Doctor Zhivago* had thirty years earlier. Based on Boris Pasternak's novel of the Russian Revolution and civil war, that film also privileged the personal over the public. Its anti-revolutionary sentiment was viewed as part of the denunciation of communism that the West espoused. It was politically correct in its day, just like *Casablanca* was in its day. *The English Patient* is not in harmony with official sentiment. It is out of tune with the established view of World War II and the requirements of public morality. I had been a fan of *Doctor Zhivago,* cheering the good doctor's love as I now cheer the count's and the state be damned. So somewhere inside there must be continuity. The self that I am now expressing has never left me, even during the days of ideological commitment. The anti-ideological self has always been there, waiting to surface.

The poet within me has meant more than the ideologist. In the public mind the role of the persona of the self-styled guru of western regionalism sticks to me because that is what I have done. Those are the ideas that I have created, my historical baggage. One does not have to be a fine poet in a public way (in terms of the quality of one's published poetry) to value the poetic voice over the political voice. This is an internal decision, an internal valuing. The quest of radical regionalism and the creation of a society based on an ideology of indigenous socialism has become history. The trajectory of a personally conceived project remains unrealized. While a politician like Preston Manning can survey his political accomplishments, an intellectual like myself can only deliver ideas. When those ideas, offered to the world as non-fiction, are turned by real history into a fiction, the creator of those ideas can only obtain revenge by fictionalizing history, espousing personal truth in the face of history's horror. *Casablanca, Doctor Zhivago* and *The English Patient* are all fictional stories about the battle between the individual and history, private love and public duty, the personal and the social. For the writer as poet rather than the writer as ideologist, the personal is the core of the story. It is that story that awaits me.

———————————

RADICAL REGIONALISM

The cover of Radical Regionalism *(NeWest, 1981).*

Rivers of the Mind:
Praying to Water

WRITERS' MINDS ARE NOT THEIR OWN. THEY view the world as a universe alive with mystery. They tingle with all the externality created by sight, smell and touch. Writers' minds flow like water (the famous stream of consciousness), sometimes fast, sometimes slow, always carrying curious bits of debris from other places, from the past into the present. And yet writers' minds, as they create words and ideas, seem so internal, so inside, a voice our own and yet not our own— linked precariously to the space and time we occupy. This link between the external and the internal, the outside and the inside is a mental landscape that shapes the mind into a river flowing with constant metaphors. My relationship to the Bow River in Calgary is such a metaphor.

It is a relationship alive with the delights of a world framed by imagination and symbol, where exploration never ends and meaning keeps unfolding. Like the river itself, it never stops. For too long we in Western Canada have been dominated by the image of the land, by which we mean the soil, the landscape, the great vistas of prairie and mountain. The land is both the great psychic reality of the region in which we live and it is also our great metaphor. Whether we imagine the great thundering herds of bison that roamed Alberta two centuries ago or the sunburnt farmer on his tractor, we Westerners identify with "the land." In this overpowering cultural icon, rivers are few and far between, hidden below the line of horizon, forgotten by our sight. If we examine the works of outstanding Western essayists, seeking to find an image other than one of the land, we will generally be disappointed.

In Stan Rowe's *Home Place: Essays on Ecology,* there is grass as far as the eye can see. The only thing mentioned about water is its lack. Don Gayton's wonderful book *The Wheatgrass Mechanism: Science and Imagination in the Western Canadian Landscape* has a creek but no rivers. An earlier book, *Silton Seasons* by R. D. Symons, speaks eloquently about country life. There is a bit of a lake in it, but that is it for water. All these essayists are from Saskatchewan, whose southern part is sorely lacking in rivers. Southern Alberta is only slightly better off, but Alberta essayists have found an affinity for rivers that their Saskatchewan colleagues have not. The great prairie novelist Rudy Wiebe wrote a book called *Playing Dead: A Contemplation Concerning the Arctic* in which rivers are central. He turned his gaze to northern Alberta and beyond and found water everywhere. But his gaze went beyond our imaginary landscape. The same occurred for Kevin Van Tighem, whose collection of essays, *Coming West: A Natural History of Home,* articulates the importance of rivers to the southern Alberta psyche. Alberta writers seem to be drawn to water. I'm one of them. In fact, my relationship with the Bow is central to my identity as an Albertan, which may seem a bit unusual, but, of course, writers should be unusual.

We humans are creatures of the land, only occasionally venturing into the alien terrain we call water. In recent history, people came West to farm the land, to turn the dry prairie land-scape into a livelihood. Only the Icelanders came to central Manitoba to fish Lake Winnipeg. The parkland that divides the prairie south from the boreal forest of the north was also settled because it provided wood for shelter and heat, but, in general, the lake- and river-filled north of the pre-Cambrian shield was avoided because it had no potential for agriculture. As a result lakes and rivers retreated from our mental landscape. The stereotype of the flat, dry prairie land became our dominant image.

We usually forget that our bodies are primarily water, and we completely ignore the importance of air to our minute-to-minute existence. Air and water are taken for granted, while our minds consciously identify with the stability of the land beneath our feet. The moving waters of a river make us nervous and cautious. From childhood we are warned about the dangers of drowning or of falling through the winter ice. To view a river as profoundly as we view the land is truly something very special, unusual because the land is our natural home. To identify with a river is to be somehow unnatural, especially for a Westerner.

Many years ago I produced a small woodcut, which I titled "The People Are a River in the Land," which was intended to symbolize the flow of human history within the Western landscape. I was inspired to create this image when I lived by the banks of the North Saskatchewan River in Edmonton. That river and its valley were the focal point of my personal geography while I lived in that city. The valley provided me with an alternative, natural sense of place in contrast to the concrete streets and house-lined sidewalks of the city. Its spruce-filled ravines, which fed into the river, carried me on narrow, winding footpaths that were cool and shaded in summer and great for skiing in winter. The sky opened up in the valley, transporting me to another

THE PEOPLE ARE
A RIVER IN THE LAND

Woodcut by George Melnyk, 1975.

realm, a communion with Edmonton's fur-trading past and with everything natural rather than human-made. The space created by the river provided my mind with a sense of eternity, which the city could never do.

The importance of rivers to my prairie mind is rooted in childhood, when imaginations are formed and symbols and metaphors curl deep in our psyche. As a young boy growing up in Winnipeg I would often go down to the banks of the Red River near our home to catch bullheads or simply to watch the sticks I threw in the water float away. There was a freedom on the bank of the river that no other place could give me. The river replaced the humdrum of home and school with risk and danger. It gave me a sense of another self, a different personhood. On the river I could freely imagine.

This boyhood connection to water had started even earlier in a kind of baptism, whose details I no longer remember. As a child only four years old, I experienced the great Noahan flood that engulfed Winnipeg in 1950. That event wed me forever to rivers and water. (Today, there is a copy of a picture book on our coffee table about another great Manitoba flood, the "Red Sea" of 1997.) Every summer my parents would take my brother and me to Lake Winnipeg to go swimming at one of the beaches. The lake was the exit point for the Red River, which flowed through Winnipeg, and whenever I return to the city of my childhood I usually visit a beach or a lake as well. When we were very young it was the family custom to spend a Sunday afternoon at Assiniboine Park, along the river of the same name. The Red and Assiniboine come together in Winnipeg, creating a meeting place, a focal point for human activity. It is not surprising that I should end up living in a city like Calgary, where two rivers also meet.

When I first moved to Calgary I remember going swimming in the Bow on the outskirts of the city at Bowness Park. My brother was visiting from Europe at the time and he insisted that we do this. As I entered the cold mountain-fed water and felt the great power of the current I knew the river had baptised me a Calgarian. My Winnipeg world repeated itself in Calgary. As a boy I followed the Red River to Lake Winnipeg either by train or in a car, and I now follow the Bow to Banff and the great expanse of mountain wilderness that is as formidable as the vast, wide and wild waters of Lake Winnipeg, an inland sea. In this way the lines drawn by rivers have become the compass points of my soul, without which I would be lost in secular urbanity. When I view a river I do not think of recreation, entertainment or even beauty. I think of the sacred role of rivers in my life.

The meaning of a river can only be grasped through our imagination. Upbringing has provided us with unique stories and symbols that allow us to communicate with rivers and to understand them and what they are saying to us in our own, unique way. Our personal history and the history of the river meet in our minds. To touch the spirit of a river means making it part of our spirit. This requires our going beyond our culture's treatment of rivers as environmental battlegrounds or as simple objects of natural beauty. We need a personal communion with a river that will bring magic to our lives. Without such mystery we are left with function and use, the preserve of technical writers.

A river should call us to poetry. Some years ago when I was visiting Saskatchewan on a research and writing project, I would regularly find myself on the banks of the South Saskatchewan River north of Swift Current. In summer I would always stop at the river and go for a swim. As soon as I entered the water I felt connected to my home in Calgary 500 kilometres away. It was the same water. I felt welcome in a familiar world. It was a feeling that no cell phone can replicate. The river was here for me, making me feel profoundly at home.

When I stayed in Saskatoon one winter to work on the same project, I made sure that I lived near the South Saskatchewan River. I stayed with friends and walked along the riverbank's snow-covered footpaths to the university, where I was working. The experience re-enacted my walking to work along the bluff that leads from my home in Calgary to where I worked on the Bow.

Historically, the rivers of the West were the great transportation routes of earlier centuries. They created the basic paradigm of western expansion. The northeasterly flow of Alberta's rivers has defined us as much as the southeasterly flow of the Missouri has the American West. That definition is not just history. It can be real today. Even though the rivers are no longer the corridors of trade and transportation that they were in the fur-trade era, they are the lifeblood of urban centres. In the case of Edmonton, Calgary and Saskatoon they are the source of water without which neither inhabitants nor industry survive.

In regaining a sense of importance for rivers we go beyond history, economics or sociology. We return to them as sacred source, a spiritual reality that is as important to our existence and happiness as all the products of civilization. In today's urban universe, the river that flows through our city gives us the images, the symbols, the space and time to be at peace. Rivers of the mind add to our souls, while the paraphernalia of ordinary existence subtracts.

The Bow is now the river of life for me. Not long ago I was diagnosed with a heart ailment. In the process of coming to terms with the news I turned to the river for inspiration. I went down to it and imagined that its strong current was the same as the flow of blood in my heart. I would sing the praises of the river and so of my heart. I never fail to speak to the river when I cross it and to offer it a prayer. My mind has found a power in the river that keeps me alive, at least mentally. The metaphor of the river's flow has connected the external world and my internal world in a unity I would not otherwise have.

It is as important to talk to rivers as it is to talk to doctors. A prayerful stance before a river, an acceptance of the great gift that it is for all living things that depend on it, is a way of keeping the sacred in the city. The seasons of a river, with its high-energy spring, its low-energy summer and its hidden winter, are the way we humans live—sometimes full of creativity, sometimes passive and slow. Rivers are metaphors for our lives, our moods, our emotions, our dreams. Ever since I was a boy, water has been the place where imagination made itself felt.

It is not just wild, free-flowing rivers that stir the imagination and lead us to self-understanding. It can be dammed and polluted rivers as well. More than forty years ago my father took me down to the Red River and told me how gigantic sturgeon had once lived in it. Somewhere on the muddy bottom that I couldn't see was the home of prehistoric creatures that made the existence of human beings a minor speck in time. A boy never forgets these dragons. They live on inside him. Rivers are full of wisdom and insight and through telling their stories we keep them alive. If we don't, then they become expendable, without significance.

Rivers are viewed by many different eyes and experienced in many different ways. When I walk across the bridges that span the Bow in downtown Calgary I always feel the wind on my face, reminding me of the westerly mountains where it comes from. The wind speaks to me of human fragility, of the great power of nature. It is always humbling to cross the river. The river of the mind can be both welcoming and frightening, comforting and threatening, peaceful or aggressive. Its contradictoriness is based on our own contradictory nature because we are its imaginers.

A long time ago in a book titled *Radical Regionalism,* I wrote about how water and steel were the two main symbols of my existence, the one representing softness and natural life and the other hardness and civilization. In time I have come to value the softness of rivers over the hardness of steel. Yet in my life the river and the city are Siamese twins connected at the navel. The river in the city and the city that surrounds a river are two opposed worlds that create a single world. I am trapped in this marvellous complementary duality. Without the river in the land I couldn't exist as a Western writer and a human being. It is through rivers that I have become everything that I am, and it is to rivers that I give back whatever essence I can offer.

———————————

Postscript: *On the morning of the summer day I finished editing this manuscript I got on my dark blue mountain bike, Hannibal, and rode thirteen kilometres along Calgary's Bow River valley trail system to Beaver Dam Flats to pick Saskatoons. It was a bumper crop year and I was thrilled to be out plucking berries as greedily as a hungry bear until my fingertips were stained blue with berry juice. Their colour reminded me of the blue ink from leaky fountain pens that stained my hands when I first began to write thirty years ago. The river valley gave me this gift of berries and mixed the colours of nature with the colours of culture. The transparent blue of the Bow River glistening in the morning sun, the deep dark blue of the ripe berries and the clear blue sky came together to flow over my writer's hands like Waterman's blue ink. The river had blessed me.*

Endnotes

1   This essay appeared in George Melnyk, *Radical Regionalism* (Edmonton: NeWest Press, 1981).

2   Melnyk, *Radical Regionalism* p. 45.

3   George Woodcock, *The Monk and His Message* (Vancouver: Douglas & McIntyre, 1992) p. 1.

4   Ibid. p. 14.

5   Paul Ricoeur, *The Rule of Metaphor* (Toronto: University of Toronto Press, 1977) p. 22.

6   Alvin and Heidi Toffler, *War and Anti-War* (Boston: Little, Brown, 1993) p. 22.

7   Phyllis Webb, *Nothing But Brush Strokes: Selected Prose* (Edmonton: NeWest Press, 1995) p. 99.

8   Sir William Francis Butler, *The Great Lone Land* (Toronto: Macmillan, 1970) p. 133.

9   George Melnyk, *Ribstones* (Victoria: Ekstasis Editions, 1996) p. 57.

10 Sir William Francis Butler, *The Wild North Land* (Toronto: Macmillan, 1910) p. 22.

11 Lawrence Ricou, *Vertical Man / Horizontal World: Man and Landscape in Canadian Prairie Fiction* (Vancouver: University of British Columbia Press, 1973) p. 137.

12 Sir William Francis Butler, *Sir William Butler* (London: Constable & Co., 1911) p. 254.

13 Melnyk, *Radical Regionalism.*

14 Edward McCourt, *Remember Butler*
(Toronto: McClelland & Stewart, 1967) p. 258.

15 Webb, *Nothing But Brush Strokes,* p. 101.

16 Francis W. Kaye and Robert Thacker, "Gone Back
to Alberta: Robert Kroetsch Rewriting the Great Plains" in
Great Plains Quarterly 14 (Summer 1994) pp. 167 and 176.

17 Robert Kroetsch, "On Being an Alberta Writer"
in *Open Letter* 4 (Spring 1983) p. 75.

18 Robert Kroetsch, *A Likely Story: The Writing Life*
(Red Deer: Red Deer College Press, 1995) p. 82.

19 Steiner Kvale, "Theories of Postmodernity" in Walter Truett
Anderson, ed., *The Truth About Truth: De-confusing and
Re-constructing the Postmodern World* (New York: Putnam,
1995) p. 19.

20 Linda Hutcheon, *The Politics of the Postmodern*
(New York: Routledge, 1989) p. 143.

21 James Hillman, *The Soul's Code*
(New York: Random House, 1996) p. 178.

22 Ibid. p. 189.

23 Sharon Butala, *The Perfection of the Morning:
An Apprenticeship in Nature*
(Toronto: HarperCollins, 1994) pp. 170 and 216.

24 Ibid. p. 216.

25 McCourt, *Remember Butler,* p. xi.

26 Melnyk, *Ribstones,* p. 17.

27 For a fuller discussion of the concept, see "The Metis Metaphor" in Melnyk, *Radical Regionalism.*

28 Alan F. J. Artibise, "Exploring the North American West: A Comparative Perspective" in *The American Review of Canadian Studies,* vol. 14, no.1 (Spring 1984).

29 J. M. S. Careless, "Aspects of Urban Life in the West, 1870–1914" in G. A. Stelter and A. F. J. Artibise, eds., *The Canadian City: Essays in Urban History* (Toronto: McClelland & Stewart, 1977) p. 127.

30 J. M. S. Careless, "Metropolitan and Region: The Interplay Between City and Region in Canadian History before 1914" in *Urban History Review,* vol. 78, no. 2: pp. 117–118.

31 Tom Nairn, *Faces of Nationalism: Janus Revisited* (London: Verso, 1997) p. 72.

32 Careless, "Aspects of Urban Life in the West," p. 126.

33 Careless, "Aspects of Urban Life in the West," p. 125.

34 Ibid.

35 See Richard J. Huyda, *Camera in the Interior: H. L. Hime Photographer* (Toronto: Coachhouse Press, 1975).

36 Neil Seigfried, "The Westward Shift of Manufacturing on the Prairies" in *Prairie Forum,* vol. 11, no.1 (Spring 1986) p. 87.

37 Artibise, "Exploring the North American West," p. 23.

38 Artibise, "Exploring the North American West," p. 25.

39 Paul Voisey, "The Urbanization of the Canadian Prairies 1871–1916" in R. D. Francis and H. Palmer, eds., *The Prairie West: Historical Readings* (Edmonton: University of Alberta Press, 1985) p. 385.

40 Ibid. p. 389.

41 Ibid. p. 390.

42 Ibid. p. 392.

43 Alan F. J. Artibise, "Canada as an Urban Nation" in *Daedalus* vol. 117, no. 4 (Fall 1988) p. 237.

44 Butala, *The Perfection of the Morning*, p. 60.

45 Ian Adam, "Iconicity and the Place of Butala's 'The Prize,'" in *Studies in Canadian Literature* 23:1 (1998) pp. 178-189.

46 Adam, "Iconicity," p. 186.

47 Butala, *Perfection of the Morning*, p. 203.

48 Mircea Eliade, *The Myth of the Eternal Return or, Cosmos and History* (Princeton: Princeton University Press, 1971) p. 9.

49 Ibid. p. 15.

50 Lorne Dietrick, "Memoirs of a Co-operative Farmer" (Unpublished manuscript) p. 24. Courtesy of author.

51 Ibid. p. 40.

52 *Family Herald*, February 1958.

53 Dietrick, "Memoirs," p. 51.

54 Ibid. p. 99.

55 The era of continentalist regionalism was described in the introduction to George Melnyk, *Riel to Reform: A History of Protest in Western Canada* (Saskatoon: Fifth House Publishers, 1992) p. 9.

ABOUT THE AUTHOR

George Melnyk teaches Canadian Studies at the University of Calgary. A lifetime in Western Canada has resulted in a number of books about the region, including *Radical Regionalism* (1981), *Riel to Reform: A History of Protest in Western Canada* (1992), and *Beyond Alienation: Political Essays on the West* (1993). For the past five years he has been preparing his major work, *The Literary History of Alberta*. The first volume was published in 1998 and the second came out in 1999. In the 1970s, Melnyk founded the periodical *NeWest Review* and NeWest Press, both of which were devoted to Western Canadian writing. He then became the first executive director of the Alberta Foundation for the Literary Arts and served as president of the Writers Guild of Alberta. He lives with his family in Calgary, where he dreams of riding his mountain bike to the ocean. Photo: Julia Melnyk.